ANCHOR BOOKS

THE MARCHING OF TIME

Edited by

David Foskett

First published in Great Britain in 1996 by
ANCHOR BOOKS
1-2 Wainman Road, Woodston,
Peterborough, PE2 7BU

HB ISBN 1 85930 387 0
SB ISBN 1 85930 382 X

Foreword

Anchor Books is a small press, established in 1992, with the aim of promoting readable poetry to as wide an audience as possible.

We hope to establish an outlet for writers of poetry who may have struggled to see their work in print.

The poems presented here have been selected from many entries. Editing proved to be a difficult and daunting task and as the Editor, the final selection was mine.

As time marches on do you ever stop to think about what is just around the corner? Do you sit and think about those happy childhood days getting further and further away?

All the poets included in this inspiring anthology have penned down their thoughts and feelings about the present day, and the not so distant future, also they have penned down their memories about their past.

So as we all have thoughts on the future and memories of the past, I am sure you will all be able to relate to the wide variety of poetry included. So sit back and be prepared to travel through the ages of time . . .

I trust this selection will delight and please the authors and all those who enjoy reading poetry.

David Foskett
Editor

CONTENTS

THE BEST AGE

We have come a long way
since 1823 and life in the slow lane
with their crinoline gowns
and dances on the town.
I wonder what they would say
to our burgers in a bun
and life in the fast lane.
What can we advertise
about this world we live in today,
with cars, buses and high speed trains.
This live today and pay later syndromes
would not go down well
in their posh stately run homes.
Each age professes to be
the best age.
I firmly believe today is only as good as you can make it.
If nothing else at least we are free,
to live and make choices.
Would we swap places
to go back and hear their voices,
their opinions and critics of our life.
I don't think so, I would like to say,
I am happy to be me,
to wear my T-shirt and jeans
and take life as it comes
in my front door each day.

R Medland

WHEN I WAS A KID

When I was a kid it was such fun playing games out with my brothers,
Football, cricket, hide and seek along with all the others,
Going out for walks with lemonade and some broken biscuits,
Scrumping apples from the trees, who were brave enough to risk it?
Roaring fires on bonfire night with sausages and hot potato,
Jack-in-the-box and Catherine wheels and the skies were all aglow,
Mum well she was always there to tend to our cuts and bruises,
And pulling out old cardigans to put wool to better uses,
Dad always in the garden planting out his carrots and peas,
But finding time to play with us and care for all our needs,
Christmas morning was wonderland with a stocking for each of us,
For me a doll with long hair, for my brothers a red toy bus,
Now I'm grown and have a husband and children of my own,
A nice garden with flowers in and a beautiful little home,
But I keep my thoughts in my heart and of them I would not rid,
Because I always remember the happy times of when I was just a kid.

Julie Block

DREAMS

Dreams are the wishes of the heart
For you my dreams I will impart,
My hopes for the future I will lay bare
My innermost thoughts for you to share,
I long for a world, maybe in our time
When peace will reign forever sublime,
Love and trust alone will hold the key
To the kind of world I'd like to see,
Children of all races happily at play
Without any fear to get in the way,
No longer lives to be held so cheap
There'd be none left behind to sorrow and weep,
If you wish hard enough maybe dreams do come true
So I'll go on wishing, perhaps you will too.

Audrey K Price

REMINISCING

I see a small child
Of aged three or four
Can't reach the doorbell
So knocks on the door

I see a child
Of aged seven or eight
Jumping over the wall
Never using the gate

I see a child
Of teenage years
Pimples and spots
And plenty of tears

I see a young adult
Learning about life
Boyfriends and girlfriends
Causing nothing but strife

The coming of age
That is, twenty one
Where is my childhood,
My youth, it's all gone

Thirties and forties
Yet to come
There's still time to be
A dad or a mum

Fifties and sixties
The kids all left home
Plenty of time now
To reminisce on our own.

L M Townend

THAT SPECIAL PLACE

Twelve months have now gone dear,
A lonely year it's true,
Not one single day has passed,
I didn't think of you.

Often sat here lonely,
And cried, and cried, and cried,
Didn't want to live here,
Without you by my side.

Somehow I felt you by me,
Giving courage to carry on,
So I trod the road without you,
Because you said go on.

Many new friends I have found now,
To give me hope it's true,
They talk and walk beside me,
So I've told them all of you.

Don't know when we'll meet again,
Not even time or place,
So I'll keep you in my heart dear,
In that very special place.

G W Bailey

LONER

In season, marbles bowled into cricket,
Leapfrog bounced into football.
Kites and fights skittered between.
Every classroom spelled chalk,
Wet clothing, teacher's canes.
He walked away.

Who needs a place? Just
Body, mind and space to dream.
Travelling time as a fish
Travels water, left no marks.
Scratched no memories.
Left no footprints.

Geoff Gaskill

MILLER'S DREAM

The old mill by the stream,
ripples forth a miller's dream,
the water is pure and clear,
pebbles lay on the bed quit near,
the old church stands near by,
rings its bells with a loud cry,
quaint cottages stand in a row,
window boxes give a good show,
all the pretty flowers give colour,
complemented with one another,
old dirt roads are unspoiled,
for walkers and horses there is no toil,
few little shops are on the corner,
display goods outside for all to wonder,
shopkeepers in long aprons and straw hat,
welcome each one with a friendly chat,
the old mill wheels turn around,
touching the water as they go round,
preparing flour for making fresh bread,
to lay on our table with butter to spread.

Teresa J Walker

MR JOHNSON
(Hero unsung - died 1921)

He stayed with us that long hot summer, then
Living in a bell ten on the lea.
My Grandma saw to his needs - that sick man,
His lungs destroyed. He made a friend of me.

In that green pleasant field behind our house
Where giant dog daisies grew around his tent,
He had a bed, a table, and a couch
In his canvas dwelling, where each day I went.

I cannot now recall the things he said -
But remember him, thoughtful - so very kind.
The days of that summer then quickly fled -
With my chatter, his manner quiet - resigned.

I recall now the night, I was in bed:
I heard my Grandma say 'Where is the boy?
He wants to see him, a last chat to enjoy.'
But Dad replied: 'No! It is much too late.'
Then in the night there passed death's shadow - fate!

Next morning to the field, so sweet with hay,
I went to see if he was still abed.
But there in silence on his couch he lay,
And I, then only four - knew he was dead!

Jack Judd

MEMORIES OF YESTERYEAR

In days of yesteryear, we always had to walk,
We were allowed to listen, but never to talk
There was no junk food then, our Mother cooked a lot,
That lasted us for days, that's all that we had got.
We didn't have a bathroom just a toilet in the yard.
Going in the cold at night, was so very hard.
Our little coal fire would be burning in the grate
No heating upstairs, that we used to hate
As for entertainments, no radio nor TV
Mother played the organ, while we sang in harmony,
Always a friendly atmosphere, neighbours helped each other
Us kids run the errands, for someone's elderly mother
We had to respect elders, and their property
If ever naughty, then we had no tea,
The horse roads were quiet, and there we could play
No fear of being run over, we could stay all day
Then when we were old enough, the thoughts of leaving school,
Finding a job, well that was the rule
Picking up our pay packet, giving it to Mam
Had a penny back for a ride on the tram
No thoughts of rape, muggings or drugs
We stayed home at nights, making rag rugs
As we got older, time for our first date
Dreaming at night about our future wedded mate
Life was gentle then, never any speed.
That was for years, then came the *greed.*

Joan Jeffries

BONFIRE NIGHT

To see a real bonfire today is oh so rare
No flames dancing and smoke in the air.
Roast potatoes, parkin and toffee apples too
Things of the past, it's now the barbecue
Hot dogs and sticky toffee are made no more
Mum goes and buys them at the local store.
No potatoes roasting in the dying embers.
It's only us old cronies that remembers
Those past days of the fifth of November -
When we as children dragged our wood
We would fetch and carry as much as we could
Stacked upon spare land as high as we might
We even had someone guarding it each night.
Making our Guy Fawkes with cast-off rags
Stuffing him with leaves and old paper bags.
"Penny for the Guy sir," was our plea
I mean the old penny, not 1p.
That really was the best event
When the money we collected on fireworks we spent.
The bonfire was usually lit around six.
As we would all gather around still piling on sticks.
Still smouldering the very next day at dawn
We would sneak a look before school that next morn
But no one seems to bother any more
Another old custom gone out the door
The only thing that remains just the same
The fire engine is its name
Those bells all silenced are no more
Just loud sirens screeching noisily past our door.

Yvonne Monks

THE SIXTIES

I spent my teens in the sixties
When everything seemed great
Everyone seemed so carefree
I'm sure there was far less hate

And of course there were The Beatles
Their songs took over the charts
John, Paul, George and Ringo
They went right to our hearts

The mods and rockers hit the scene
Rivals they were to be sure
On their scooters and their motor-bikes
Along roadways they would roar

We had such laughs, such wonderful fun
We enjoyed life to the full
Everywhere was bright and cheerful
Nowhere I am sure was dull

Dances were always so popular
We would go on a Saturday night
In bell-bottom trousers and mini-skirts
Granddad shirts and lacy tights

We'd twist, we'd shake and do the jive
Moving all over the floor
Stopping to drink our lager and lime
Then dancing around lots more

Unpleasant things did happen of course
But we were too young to care
We were much too busy enjoying ourselves
And building 'castles in the air'.

Jill Campbell

IN PRAISE OF A LILY

From earth's brown dungeon
You pushed your way
So uncurl your fronds
In the light of day
To raise your face
To sunlit rays
And fill the air
With exquisite bouquets
More regal than Solomon
The Lord spoke your name
To give us a message
It gave you fame
We don't need to worry
What tomorrow will bring
He cares for us so
We just ought to sing
Despite wars and strife
The future is bright
For God's in his heaven
The world will be alright

Olive Crombie

PAST, PRESENT AND FUTURE

Time is life, and the clock is ticking fast,
time to bury the past.
Live your moments, then make room for the future,
don't let old regrets get a chance to last.

The past should have a place in your memory, but not felt,
previous wounds can easily open again and sting deep.
On the present time you should concentrate,
forget all the things that make you weep.

The future holds more tasks and hurdles to confront,
nothing can change if a part of you is still lingering behind.
To deal with the life ahead you must give yourself,
that means the whole of your heart and mind.

Without it the past will haunt you endlessly,
the future will always seem dull and bleak.
Deal with what it is that hurts you at the time,
don't live your life feeling weak.

Lee West

REMEMBERING

I use to walk in fields of green
tall trees and birds all types to
be seen the gentle flow of a
winding stream, where I could
lie and dream of girlish romantic things.

And now many years have passed
towering buildings stand instead
of trees and concrete yards
replace the grass.

And yet amidst those towering
blocks the little birds still flock
reminding me of those years
now gone as they sing out their
sweet songs.

Yes I remember that winding
stream and a young girl
with her wild romantic dreams.

E Noyes

THE DAYS GONE BY

Oh how I long for the days gone by
'What has this world come to' I sigh
With drugs and violence and lots of crime
If only we could go back in time

I remember the days when I was a lass
With my family we'd picnic on the grass
Then we would lie and lap up the sun
The simple things in life were fun

In those days there was no TV
But we were happy as could be
We'd sit around the table and talk
I'd draw on my blackboard with my chalk

We'd play at scrabble or some other game
The next night we may play the same
We'd all sit around a lovely coal fire
Then mother would kiss us before we'd retire

I'd get the strap which would hurt my pride
But mother she'd take the teacher's side
'You must have deserved it' she would say
'So don't come crying to me today'

For adults we were taught respect
Good manners we must never neglect
'Sometimes these things are forgotten' I cry
Oh how I long for the days gone by

Janet McBride

FIGHTING FOR THE WRONG

We fought for our freedom, we chose to vote
We sacrificed our liberty, for something we didn't know
We struggled to be proven, we rose to the challenge
And now we moan that we just can't manage

We asked for equal rights, we wanted to be, someone
We had to show our worth, we wanted to have some fun
How far we came, how much we gained
And now we wish it was like the old days again

Did we want too much to be a person
To be looked upon with pride and respect
And now we see that the damage is done
How our lives are so different, how much it can affect.

Jacqui Simpkin

DUTCH COTTAGE

Just off the island road,
A Dutch cottage built in sixteen eighteen,
Stands alone, with wooden garden fence
and white flag pole, surrounded by
flower beds, trees and bright green lawns.

A museum she had become,

Relics of the past can be seen,
Placed throughout her grounds,
She has a good thatched roof,
with little windows,
small walls and a solid door.

A building protected by legislation,
which will still stand there
for future generations.

G F Snook

CHANGING VALUES

There was a time, some years ago
When every face you seemed to know
When people had the time to spare
A kindly word to show they care
Doors left unlocked both night and day
No fear, no evil to keep at bay
The word *respect* springs to mind
Respect today is hard to find
No longer safe to walk the street
Without listening out for following feet
And when you've reached the twilight years
You should not have shed some tears
Just because you're easy prey
For some young thug who comes your way
They seem to think what's yours is mine
Never once showing the slightest sign
Of *respect*, that should be shown to all
So we all put up a great big wall
Becoming faceless to keep away
Those with no respect for others today

S M Sutton

GERRY AND THE PEACEMAKERS

As they walk through the storm
Looking up to the sky
They will see the light through the dark

There are doves in the air
And no longer despair
Now at last, men of peace make their mark

Walk on, take the strain!
Walk on, through the pain!

May their efforts bear fruit we pray ... we pray

Adams, Bruton! Clinton . . . Major!
Hold your heads up high . . . high!

Walk on! Walk on!
Walk on . . . Walk on!

Lets all give peace a try!

Stephen Friede

THE LAST LIBRETTO

Who hears the horses' hooves flying
towards our planet dying?
Who cares the Four Horsemen ride
as Lucifer lengthens his stride?
Ever nearer the hoof beats pound,
who heeds their warning sound?
We have raped the earth
that gave us birth,
polluted the sky,
left creatures to die.
Can we face a future here
without pardon or fear?
Yesterday was the parent
of today's discontent
still it is not too late
to stem a dismal fate.
We build our lives on shifting sand
leading us to a nether land.
We alone ourselves betray
while hedonism rules the day.
Time still to change our ways
and safeguard future days,
before the last bird sings
or the last bell rings.

Anna Punshon

STEPPING BACK IN TIME

As I sit and reminisce in my fireside chair
Or on a warm day sat out in the garden in the fresh air,
Stepping back in time and those memorabilia days long gone,
Living once again over those childhood and romantic times that shone,
Remembering mostly the happy and carefree ones, not the bad
And thanking God for his kindness, also helping with the sad,
Together with life's traumas and tribulations with the ability to cope,
The gift of faithfulness and encouragement not to give up hope.
Life appeared less hectic during those early days of the century,
The placid and contented way of life seemed quite elementary.
Then in the nineteen thirties times became more trendy,
The Victorian and steam age were replaced with automobiles and
Yanky Doodle Dandies.
The decades of nostalgia and changing scenes
Some welcomed, some feared or what might have been,
Is an aspect of life which we have to accept
And resign ourselves peacefully without contempt.
Some say we have to change with the times, come what may,
Perhaps not always for the better which is the price we pay,
For the advancements which have been created
But it is nice to still remember those tender memories and the old ways,
now out dated.
The nineteen eighties brought many different things on to the human race
course
With new technology advancing fast and machines taking over the work force.
I suppose as H G Wells quoted in his book 'The shape of things to come'
Will always be and understood by some.
Now in the last decade of the century the computer age we see,
Whatever will be next in store after the year 2000 AD
And I wonder if our ancestors would have agreed or intervened
If they were just a number fed into a machine,
But as I sit in my garden and watch those plants grow and bloom so dear,
I thank God we cannot change nature or the seasons in the year.

Nancy Owen

SUPERMARKET

When I was young we local shopped there was no supermarket
We took the car we hadn't got 'cos there was nowhere to park it
But things have changed and most of us, can shop just where we please
For packet, bottle, jar or bag, pre-packed bacon and some cheese

Outside you choose a trolley and I've often heard it said
They manufacture all of them, each with a gammy leg
You set your sight, and hold your breath, arms rigid then take aim
But then go round in circles as if suddenly struck down lame

You set off down the aisle, each side, displays some packaged fare
The price now marked in kilograms, gives some old girl a scare
It used to be two fifty and it's now priced near six quid
It's quantified by it was, now is, on a sticker on the lid

You can't see what you're looking for, as all the colours gel
We've missed this one, and that one too come back for that as well
We've travelled through the maze with very little in the cart
We've missed so many items let's go back down to the start

The special offers tickle me buy two at half the price
Of course that's not exactly true should I have said it's thrice
Do they jack up the price, then slash it by, say fifty percent
So that it looks a super deal a gift from heaven sent

Another special offer, evolves from the sell by date
If you were having visitors would you put it on their plate
The fact that it's run out of time, and consideration for my health
As it's only ten pence off I will leave it on the shelf

One thing's clear if you do shop from store to store with thrift
Eventually, calculator held, and time, some pence you'll lift
But if you've travelled carefully, still, petrol needle in the red
You haven't saved, though thought you had, got it well 'nuff said

C B Sutton

NOT FOR SALE

I can't begin to tell you
About my new abode
It's on the edge of countryside
Down a quiet little road,
When I first stepped through the door
I knew it was for me
The view was really brilliant
Only thing missing was the sea,
Its style is really quite unique
And there are no stairs to climb
All the hoovering and dusting
Are done in half the time,
Outside in the garden
There are roses all around,
Relaxing on the patio
You never hear a sound,
I wish I'd lived here in the past
But the present is much alive,
I hope my future does lie here
When I'm sixty-five!

Janet Bedford

RINGING TRUE

Great Aunt Bella almost reached a hundred and one.
She'd seen so many changes since her long life had begun,
From horse-drawn carriages and war, to men walking on the moon -
She enjoyed her church, and loved the ancient hymns' sweet tunes.
She'd drunk fully from life's cup, and had the wisdom of the aged.
She'd whisper, 'See The Power and The Glory' as the wild storm raged.
She confided in me once, her clouded eyes suddenly aglow.
'The vicar is a dear, but he's quite wrong you know,
One should not stand in God's shadow - One should dance in his light.'
As time passes, I'm ever more certain that dear Aunt Bella was right.

Linda Miller

CHILD OF THE 50'S

It was school on Mondays
Church on Sundays
And jelly for Saturday tea.
We had Clarks' sandals
And ladybird tea-shirts
And Fry's 5 boys chocolate bars.
Mars bars were 4½d
And our mums made lemonade
The streams were not polluted
So we could paddle there
Trying to catch little fish.
In school we had dip-pens and ink-wells
The school dentist in the 'agony-van'.
The boys all wore knee-length grey shorts
And taught you to swear in 'sums'
We all 'played-out' at weekends
No-one stayed inside!
We skipped and played 'two-ball'
We climbed trees and walls
We played 'cowboys' and 'robbers'
We rode bikes or went sledging . . .

Oh memories like old jeans
Tend to fade and fray
But we had lots of things
That kids don't have today

Paula Weare

THE WANDERER

Another day, I stand alone,
 my friend has gone, I'm on my own,
I'm glad to say she is nearby,
 across the track, the roads, the lay-by,
She changed her job for peace of mind,
 to cut the journeys, which were a bind.
From home to Doncaster then onto Newcastle,
 a demanding job, accounts and hassle.
She worked for railways being broken up,
 a government policy, which is bankrupt.
Now my friend has peace of mind,
 anything else would be unkind.
I stand alone awaiting a train,
 the station offices are empty, no one
 to explain,
Where trains or staff, may be found,
 and each and everyone of us to confound,
that this government's policies were ultra right,
 and now in Britain, we are all onto a travel blight!

Alan Noble

HOBSON'S CHOICE

Transport the future, what will it be?
Will cars, planes be no more?
Will they build teleport stations,
To break down our molecules, to get us from A to B?

Or will they transform our present day cars
To hover, like the hovercrafts we have now?

Maybe they will invent an astronaut suit
Which will give you total control of air space!

Maybe they might make a new cross breed
Between a horse and a bird like Pegasus
To be both pollution and environmentally friendly?

Or supersonic shuttles that run on nuclear energy
Depending where we are: on earth or in space
Transport will always be changing

A M Bridgewood

SPACEMAN

They're bound to say it's all my fault
I shouldn't have bothered in the first place
Because the spaceship that I went and hired
Has broken down in outer space

I can't see me getting home tonight
Why it all happens to me
Suppose I'll have to put a space suit on
And lift the bonnet and see

It's a bit out of the way is this
Can't see any ships around
If my spanners don't float off in space
I'll soon sort it, it'll be sound

Not right up on mechanics
I'm a tonsil man myself
But I'll see if any pipes are blocked
And nurse them back to health

I don't much fancy going out there
It's pitch black I'll be alone
Maybe I'll just hang on a bit
I'm only five galaxies from home.

Fred Tighe

UNTITLED

We've advanced so fast in fifty years,
progress has taken us by storm.
But to me it spells of misery
and who'll be there to mourn?

They have taken some thing precious
they compute - but not by name.
I'm thought by them as numbers
and this progress is called gain

That does not compute inside my mind
numbers are nought to me
Rows of numbers can't have feelings
nor can they sigh or see.

My name means I am some-one
So my name it must remain
Nought does the computer think of me
but with a name 'tis not the same.

Each name says it's a some-one,
a row of numbers leaves a blank.
With numbers there's no body
and 'tis progress we must thank.

So when I'm told my number's up
I'll say 'tis a mistake
'Cos I'm no number, I'm a person
that you can't irradicate.

O take me back those fifty years
so's they call me by my name
Progress thinks of me as numbers
and it really ain't the same.

Rosie Hues

GONE SLEDGIN'

Hung on bent rusty nail
worn rope with tatty ends,
eager hope on which to sail
junior joy swiftly sends.

Sled in snow quickly mends
frost that bit on woodland walk,
the drench of fakes, hidden bends,
sky and sun, important fork

to golf course with no talk.
Greens and bunkers muffled white
sentinel flags mark my balk,
boots trudged in creaking fight.

Then the slope to capture sight
a brook that chortled at the base.
Ran pushed with all might
of spurring engines in my pace,

belly dived with burning face
and met the spray of icy blast,
as runners sank to ploughing race
wellies filled with snowy cast.

Knew my sledge would come at last
beside friend's latest toys,
though I gained fun in winter fast,
with sodden socks and simple joys.

Chris Antcliff

THE WHITE PLANET

The frozen orb circles the sun
Shrouded in a blanket of snowy ice
No spring, summer or autumn
Just a cold freezing winter
No lightness comes upon the lands
Only darkness, just a cold darkness
They were warned and warned
But they would not listen
Just testing they said, just testing
Testing for a bigger and better bomb
It will do no harm they said
Now look what has happened
Our world has gone, gone forever
No life forms exist here any more
There's nothing left, only death
Our planet's gone, a lifeless sphere
Just testing they said, just testing
Now it has all gone away
This frozen earth orbiting the sun
Never to live again.

David Brownley

PHOENIX

In this City, with its ragged walls,
its tombed history and tomorrow's pardon
etched in a new language, I feel
I am bathing in a scented sea,
or walking in a scented garden.

Everything can be new if the test
of a leaping spirit or a free mind
is played upon the grey material,
distilling colours, glorious and fresh,
from the manacles that bend and bind.

Hope does not lie in a new constitution,
in the fretted image of a lost
culture, spread through books and stories;
but in the wayward attitude
that demands a kingdom and spurns cost.

John Atkins

SOUNDS OF YEARS GONE BY

The sound of the horse and cart
as it crosses the cobbled stones.
The driver calling,
'Any old rags, bottles, or bones.'
It brings out the children Oh! So quick,
to exchange their jam jars, for a balloon on a stick.
The errand boys whistling as they go on their way,
working hard, for little pay.
The Tramcar on its rails, rattling along,
The gramophone winding down, as it plays its song.
The hiss of the trains, letting off steam,
only heard now in your dreams.

Just as day is dawning,
the sound of the sirens warning.
The boom of gunfire fills the sky,
The drone of the engine, as the Doodle Bug flies by.
The silence as the engine cuts out,
The *Crash*, the debris, laying about.
The laughter of relief, to still be in one piece,
The tears of sorrow, for those with no tomorrow.
Let's pray that these sounds of war,
will stay where they belong,
In the past, *For evermore*.

Myrtle Elden

THE OLD HOME

An old man now, I sadly gaze
Remembering far off summer days.
In my thoughts I now recall
The cottage in the old stone walls.
A garden filled with rich produce
Of which my mother made good use,
With all the wholesome, home-grown fare
Our table was not ever bare.
A stone shed where the coal was stored
And logs we'd gathered from the wood,
Fire burning warmly bright
Tempered the bitter winter night.
The front laid out with beds of flowers
I loved to tend in leisure hours,
How sad to see the plot forlorn,
This ruined house, where I was born.

Owen Jones

STEAM TRAIN NOSTALGIA

I loved to ride in the steam train
As it clickety clacked along
It seemed as though it was singing
A merry little song
The fire in the engine was glowing
Sending out the steam
And then, it would blow its whistle
With a loud and piercing scream
It was so great to sit in the steam train
As the countryside sped by
I remember the days of the steam train
With a happy nostalgic sigh!

Dorothy Durrant

THE PENSIONERS' PLIGHT

Another nail in
Our coffin
And we are on
Our way.
Who cares about
The old people
Of today.

The rich sit down
And drink their tea
Do they ever think
To say
We thank thee

Just another old woman
Trying to get warm
But what about
The storms.

No money for the meters
No heat or light
We'll just have to sit
Here just another night

What will tomorrow bring.
Just another day
For us old ones
Oh no
We'll soon be on our way.

Lilian Coombs

RENDALL STREET SCHOOL
WHIP AND TOP

Making the way to school
In a haphazard zig-zag fashion along the way,
Forgetful of time . . .

Painted stick in hand with leather thong
To whip the stripy-coloured top and spin it
With the rings of beige-and-blue or yellow-and-red a-twirling . . .

Clumsy fingers eagerly twist the whip-leather tightly around the
stem of the top,

Then a stoop to the pavement to begin the spin;
And 'Swoosh'! In the air Top goes as the leather swiftly unleashes its hold . . .

Up on tip-toe so fast Top spins,
Then is whipped on unless it should fall;
And it skims and bounces with wooden tone
And a tap, tap of the nail-tip or nail-head on the pavestone ground;
And goes round and around and around and around . . .

Then boldly Top is whipped again,
And up it bounds,
And 'off the kerb' and along the road it goes . . .

And it feels one can sense a faintish humming 'hum-m-m-m-m'
With the colours of Top going all in to one in its dizziness . . .

And still on and still on and still on Top spins,
As with a 'whip', Top skips and on she skims
And hops up on tip-toe and poses there a-whirling . . .

School-bells ring in the unheeding ears of those
Impatient only to continue the play . . .

Joy within the being is a child at pleasure,
Light at heart,
No meaning to time -
All is just a motion on a moment -
All is on memory . . .

Mary Pauline Winter

WHEN I WAS YOUNG

When I was young I would walk for miles
to see my gran and one of her smiles.
I would walk down country lanes and across fields so wide
With no-one but mother nature at my side
I would sit by a stream with water so clear,
and if I kept really still, little fish would swim near,
In the spring I would pick wild violets and primroses on the way,
and take them home for Mother's Day.
I could walk by hedgerows, and past many farms,
I could walk alone and come to no harm,
I have lived in my town all my life,
and in that time I have become a mum and wife,
The country lane is now a dual carriageway.
The fields have gone, factories have come to stay.
Where the farms once stood alone and proud,
stands housing estates with children shouting loud,
I'm sad that my future grandchildren will never see,
The places that were so dear to me
but I will tell them about my special times instead
as no developers can take away the memories that are in my head.

M I Goodwin

HOT HOUSES!

The family lived in the kitchen,
The only room allowed some heat,
Round the boiler they'd warmly talk,
Together they would always eat.

The whole domestic scene was changed,
Time honoured customs were re-called,
Our cosy firesides disappeared
When central heating was installed.

With microwaves and instant food
Meal times are a thing of the past,
With heat switched on in every room,
So called progress was here to last.

Once your bedroom was where you slept,
And only stayed in when quite ill;
In the sick room you lay dosed up,
But for boredom there was no pill!

Today it's quite a different scene,
The bedroom's come into its own,
To study in or watch TV,
Or talking on your mobile phone.

Can you picture how life would be
Less instant heat and no fast food!
Now all we do is flick a switch,
We've never had it quite so good!

Mary Care

JIM REVELATIONS 1929

Erich Maria Remarque
A Boche she thought with a start
Some Englishman, Siegried Sassoon
Not in my class room
'Oh no Miss Hall, not suitable at all'
But all avidly read
'Daddy please tell' Bunty said

Uncle Jim, always cheery, gassed at Ypres
Without his throat spray couldn't speak
Nor wouldn't speak of his war, and all the things that he saw
Only once, and only one detail
'Daddy please tell'
'Very well'

Crawling along what remains of a trench
Fearful stench
Bombardment intense
Kilt all asunder, hugging wet ground
'Terrific din' said Uncle Jim
But when light came it wasn't sticky mud
But remnants of men and their blood

All this told at tea
'More jam dear?' 'No thanks, not for me'
Memories making us tense: what was the sense
Dainty life, two girls and dear wife
Daddy no more of your horrid old war

Nicholas Hutton

HOME SWEET HOME

Very oft' to mind we do recall, when we were four, consummate all.
Domicile together, harmoniously content; familiar, comfortable, consistent.
But the two we had borne were of mind, so frightful together, the quarrelsome kind;
Then miserable apart, no verbal interaction, as each missed the other, drove us to distraction.
As they matured their paths were diverse; each with their own they began to disperse.
She with the wanderlust, he with his familiar boundaries of home, nowhere spectacular.
She the gregarious, always extrovert; he the singular and quietly introvert.
Their kindred love of each other was apparent, despite their vast differences of temperament.
But when she flew the nest one day for another, he was for a while like an unrequited lover.
However her brother he was, his thoughts just sensuous (not sensual mind), his affection indeciduous
Following times together, and times apart, their family ties a binding stalwart,
His dependence on home became more tenuous; quietly he left, nothing strenuous.
Now two streets apart they continue their lives, as independents in constant strive
To be of each so more deserving, now they are grown siblings worth preserving.
We miss them both, loving each no less, and 'tis strange a remark for us to express;
For when they were home we wanted them out, and now they are gone we feel without.
But our bond is intact, stronger than ever; the web we have woven, will stay forever;
All but a gasp, a moment of breathlessness, preserved in memories of happiness.

Jennifer Wright

THE PRICE OF WAR

They played in England's meadows green,
Beneath a blue and cloudless sky,
In halcyon days of boyhood dreams,
Till war drew ever nigh.

They marched into a foreign land,
While at home the fires burned,
For the young men who answered their country's call,
And who never would return.

They fell upon the blood-soaked earth,
Where many fell before,
Wasted in the futile carnage,
Of the great and terrible war.

They perished on a foreign field,
Under a black and smoke filled sky,
The bones that remain in the reddened soil,
Now beneath the poppies lie.

They said there would be no other war,
To ever match this human cost,
But since the deaths of those gone before,
Another generation of youth has been lost.

Now, as I look upon the stone,
On which their names are carved with pride,
I feel a mother's sorrow,
For the precious sons who died.

Farewell to thee, our brave young men.
I pray you have not died in vain.
May you sleep in peace forever more,
And England see war ne'er again.

Brenda Wilding

PLEASE DON'T DO IT

I thought the British people were animal lovers
They are letting 400,000 cows get killed
Why don't they tell the Government to leave them alone
So they can peacefully graze in a field

I will eat beef any day
And ignore the ones that's trying to scare me away
I've been eating beef since I was five
After seventy years I am still much alive

According to the Government I've got twelve more years
I'm not worried I won't shed any tears
I don't mind animals being slaughtered for food
But being killed and then burnt
I think this is crude

It was man's own fault the cows got this way
It's the way man fed them every day
They fed them offal from out of sheep
That's when the disease first came into play

I feel sorry for those poor old cows
Let's hope they do find another way
But if they decide to do this awful deed
It be '*Britain's saddest day*'

We cannot call ourselves animal lovers
Not after a thing like this
Everyone should be ashamed of themselves
If those cows are burnt to a crisp

I hope in the future things work out much better
And people will help after they read my poetical letter

Bert Booley

ON BEING GIVEN AN OLD BOOK FOR A SPECIAL DAY

'You're fifty!' they shrieked,
'Fifty'
Oh boy! Fifty - years - old'
And they howled with laughter,
'The big five 0!' they spluttered.
(They were young)

'Oh I don't know,' others said.
'Fifty? Just beginning - prime of life and all that!
Don't you worry. Get *fit*, get *out there* - go for *it!' they urged.*
(They were not so young - but not fifty)

'I *am* fit. I *am* out there! I've already *gone* for it!' he shouted, 'Look at me!'
And he beat his chest . . . (and coughed.)

'Stay in there man.' cautioned the rest. 'Bend with the wind. Join us.
'Climb on board . . . (if you still can).
'It's not so bad when you're there.
Lie back, think of . . . well, not exactly England, but *you* know.
Bit of philosophy and all that . . .,' they mumbled.
(They were fifty . . . and some!)

'But age is nothing - look at this book' he argued,
'Same binding, lovely bit of skin, neat, tidy, good as new.
'Last for ever!' he bragged, 'Just like me!'
(And he wheezed a little as he coughed again.)

(But the book was twice as old - and said nothing)

Godfrey J Curtis

ECHOES OF SEASONS PAST

Merry repast with homely fare, our winter's tidings
Midnight Mass, drip dappled candles
Warm embrace our Hallowed King
Dazzle the twinkling stars cross Year End skies

Fearful future stores up rotten apples
'Mongst shiny spring freshness
Cold breezes seek out the young from old
While stark world waits upon nature's pleasure

Velvet drone bees in eloquent abundance
Pollen laden sprightly souls
Echo anew earth's message
Hovering over silver streams of light
A humming bird evokes the dance of love

On heavy scented perfumed nights
Owls fly, fox lair, the badger set
Store up, shore up - in all quick haste
Before red papier mâche leaves fall bare
Through winter's cruel fingers pointed there

Patricia Thompson

GLAD TIMES, SAD TIMES

Oh happy joyous carefree times,
Those days of yester year,
When as children we would play
With no worry or no fear.

Mothers were glad to get us out
From underneath their feet
And we would play for ever-more
Out there in the street.

With rounders, hopscotch, whip and top
We tried our best and played the lot,
The sun it seemed to always shine
We'd run and hide about bedtime.

Those days have gone, and in this age
Children seem to by pass this stage
They sit indoors, in a dreamlike stupor
Playing games on an old computer.

John J Hudson

CHAPTERS OF A LIFE . . .

Present me with my memories, and what would I see?
A mine of jumbled experiences set out before me.
Sadness and happiness, that made me what I am,
Tomorrow will hopefully only be, the 'storm before the calm'.

Present me with my life now, and what do I see?
Reflection on my youth, which I could not wait to flee.
Expectations of a child, that could not be fulfilled,
Surrendering to feelings, that were soon to be killed.
Everyone has regrets that sometimes linger in their mind,
Not letting them get a hold, is the key you will find.
Take the time to discover your worth: and be one of a kind.

Forget a past that's morbid, and look to a future that's bright,
Unlock your potential and live a life full of light.
Take your destiny in your hands, and mould it with gold,
Understand, and help others; and cultivate a wiseness of old.
Represent what you know you should, and don't live a lie -
Express the 'real' you, and enjoy the rest of your days on a high.

Lynda Miller

OUR LITTLE SHED

When I was a little girl
We had our own little shed
It sat at the bottom of the garden
beside the flower bed.
It had a blue door with windows too
We would play for hours and hours,
Clean, sweep and dress with flowers,
Pans, jugs, cups and saucers too
how comfortable and homely we would make you
Muffins, crumpets, sandwiches too,
We would make to give to you
All the children loved our shed
We would play games, and pretend
We were in bed.
The flu I think a cough or a cold
Get out the mixture and do as you are told
Two teaspoons or may be three
If you want to get better then
Listen to me,
It's getting dark, time to go in,
So close the door and be thankful, once more
What a lovely day we had
In our little shed.

Ann Smith

CHANGING GAME

I take a stroll down memory lane,
as I watch another football game.
Today they fight more than they play,
it was not like that in granddad's day.

The men wore shorts that passed their knees,
the fans could go and watch, always feeling at ease.
They look really funny, when you see them today,
but those boys really did know how to play.

Don't get me wrong, we have good players now,
and all the fans want to do, is watch their game,
without a row.
As the years have passed, lots of things have changed,
but some not as much as the football game.

Caroline Andrews

REINCARNATION

'I was born before' he said
'I've had another life,
I was once an ancient king,
With a princess for my wife.'

Under hypnotic influence
His mind was taken back,
He saw himself as in a dream
Through ages long and black.

No peasant was he worth his hire
No rags were to be seen,
But velvet, silks and ribbons
Fit for a king or queen.

No humble cottage was his home
No plain words formed his name.
His ancestors were royalty
Though we all from Adam came.

If we really had another life
Why are we kings and queens.
Does memory really play us false
Or is it just our genes?

Pauline Anderson

REMEMBRANCE

I sit, amidst the plethora of decaying vegetation,
The faint glow of summer, fading into darkness.
Beside the still water, I grip the single rose of crimson,
An isolated figure; weary, silent, motionless.
Staring at the calm, azure river in morbid retrospection,
Observing a tear-stained face on the reflected surface.
A solitary swan disturbs my thoughts of melancholy,
His head regal, his eyes filled with deserving pride.
A smile flickers across the pale features of misery,
And I toss the flower into the meandering tide.
A simple gesture, on a day, locked into my memory,
Transfixed, I watch the rose on its journey into eternity.
Then, stand with the Cathedral bells ringing in the distance,
The archaic metal peeling out the sounds of remembrance.

Steven J Smith

NEW MOON?

I see the moon,
All gods look down,
All moons see me?
No, for I am alone.
All are alone.
Never warm . . . always cold,
This desolate time.

Desolate world.
Love trips brink of new beginning,
Then for the first time
The sun can truly rise,
And the people may live
Not dream.

Dream now.
Dream that we will be free
To sing and dance and laugh.

Our hopes . . .
Our hearts . . .
Good-luck mankind.

Bill Brammar

FRUIT FOR THOUGHT

Are we to abandon our babies, as we enjoy
The mechanical things in life.
Are we to deny them beefsteak . . . and at their
Birth, present them with a fruit knife.
Are we to create two kinds of environment
In which we wish to reside?
One is 'ecological' - 'Eden' where nature is king,
And man, sustains to abide.
While the other is steel and plastic, hard-wares,
To create an easy paradise.
With machines to take the strain of our labour,
Using every conceivable device.
High thoughts, will need high action, which,
In turn with much higher cost.
Says the logic is really inescapable,
Some 'benefits' will be lost . . .
No cars to trundle in the countryside,
No holidays in someone else's sun.
Hard labour, in the fields, growing food . . .
(Is where 'technology', was hard won.)
But a degree of sensible actions, to minimise the
Overall blight of modern ways.
Give up some of the 'benefits', assess the best
Of both worlds, to lengthen our days.

Jenny Major

A CAR AND LIFE

Brought an old car to repair,
With life one can only compare.
For with each part that you renew
So your future, with it grew!

Up and running with tender loving care,
Treat people the same and they'll be fair!
With the right fuel, the engine will turn
Getting life right is now your concern.

For the highway now you must take,
Life's going right here's your break!
Choose in which lane you should drive
With lots of hard work, no time to skive!

Now you park up for a rest,
Time to relax, an answer to your quest!
So now your car stands gleaming bright,
It's fun to work and play what a delight.

So why don't you buy an old car?
For in life you can travel far!
Build it up so it can run smooth,
For you'll be happy you're back in the groove.

Penelope Ann

SONNET TO A ROCKING HORSE

Starr is my rocking horse - made long ago,
He's older than my grandpa and my nan.
Some say he's Victorian - I don't know,
Maybe he was here when the world began.

We'd go on such adventures, Starr and I,
We'd travel over mountains wild and free.
I'd climb upon his back and off we'd fly,
Or very gently canter by the sea.

I'm quite old and worn now, and so is he,
His mane and tail are very nearly gone.
The years of toil show for all to see, yet -
This dapple grey is loved by everyone.

His eyes are still bright and his smile so wide,
He'd dearly love to take you for a ride.

Wendy Preece

SHADOWS OF THE PAST

All through my life
I've been followed around
By the ghosts of the past
And the problems I've found
Look over my shoulder
And what do I see?
The mistakes that I've made
Still following me.

They say that mud sticks
And I know it's true
Why can't I forget?
What have I to do?
I made some decisions
Sometimes the wrong choice
But I live with my conscience
Everyday hear its voice.

I've made a new life
Tomorrow's a new day
But will the memories that follow
Ever go away?
I turn around now
And what do I see?
The ghosts of the past
Still following me.

Leanne Simpson

DAYS GONE BY

When I was just a little girl in 1924,
I remember coal in the cellar, ten steps below the door.
You carried an oil lamp with very great care,
To tell you the truth, I was frightened down there.

The coal was very heavy and the steps were very steep,
Better in Ireland where they have fires of peat!
The fire in the kitchen must be roaring by six,
Kindled with paper rolls and very dry sticks.

With a bit of luck the water would be nicely hot by eight,
And the big black kettle would be boiling on the grate.
Soon everyone was ready and it was off to school for us,
While father went to work by train, there was no car or bus.

We all knew the coal man, his name was Sid,
He slid the coal down the cellar grid.
But I ran to the patient horse, waiting at the gate,
Who was made to carry far too much weight.

An animal lover from an early age,
I felt within me a rush of childish rage.
I stroked his nose and gave him some clover,
I prayed that his day would soon be over.

I remember the butcher's boy delivering the meat,
Which went straight down in the cellar to make sure that it would keep.
The milk was put down there as well, where all was dark and cool,
While the baker's boy brought bread (unwrapped) before he went to school.

Fond memories of days gone by in 1924,
When I was young and coal was kept ten steps below the door.

Marguerite Bridgford

NOW! IMAGINATION OR FACT

When this you see, think of it what you will,
But make it good because we're not all made of wood.
Armies and terrorists trained to kill,
Make your thoughts positive.
Don't be easily swayed,
Drab and bleak there is little to speak.
Future like politicians heads shrouded with smog,
No jobs and other pathetic stories.
As a Nation longing to see the back of the Tories,
Papers all following each others' lead.
Royal family, politics throwing up dirt,
To sow the seed.
Businesses going down the pan,
We're a nation of also rans.
In sport and life winning is the aim,
No longer the joy of competing and working.
Cardboard cut outs making this world a total shut out,
Other Countries led by figures in the autumn of their lives.
Fall like leaves scattered by the breeze,
Starving and hungry, world wide famine.
Here, it's more simple,
Gratuitous violence on video, tough guy heroes to impersonate.
Wanting a couple of hundred to spend,
Banks reluctant to lend, repossession letters ready to send.
Driving us all round the bend,
Ram-raiding, car theft, violence on the increase.
Will it ever cease?
Social misfits carry out sickening attacks,
Who is going to take responsibility?
Children murdered and abused before life has begun,
Darkens this world forever.

David Redman

LOOKING BACK

Have you been back to childhood scenes
And thought of what might have been?
I stand, I look, I stare,
Where is my house? It's not there.

The fields where I once played
Not a stick, not a glade.
Round the bend to illusions
Ghost and memories in profusions.

Don't look back, it's not the same,
Your childhood you just can't reclaim.
Let your memories with you stay,
Just stop . . . think tomorrow is another day.

Mary Buttle

A THOUSAND TRADES MINUS ONE

The 'golden flash' and 'rocket three', das kleine wonder 'bantam',
The factory that gave them life is now an ashen phantom.
I stood and watched them pull it down . . . too young to realise,
That full grown men with callused hands, could have tears flow from their eyes.

Those halcyon days are long since passed, no more smell of sweat and toil,
No skills passed down from man to boy, no pungent smell of oil.
Condemned to death by demolition . . . a cruel and heartless fate,
Where once there lived a giant, now a mere trading estate.

I pass by there quite often, on my bike or in my car,
Recount the memories of long ago . . . the smell of 'Castrol R'.
The 'A10 twin' and 'golden star', the army's 'M21',
Will ride no more down Armoury Road for the factory's dead and gone.

I'd stand outside 'Vale Onslow's' shop for hours and simply stare,
But come the time that I could ride, well the factory was not there.
It lives only in memory, the badge of the stacked gun,
For it could not reflect the heat from the land of the rising sun.

Pete Nash

VALUABLE TIME

Essence of life, is time,
Birth, the foundation,
Development follows.
Character erases negative thoughts,
Determination, progress, pursuits.

Time allows for adolescence,
Problems occur, doubts begin.
Life can be stressful,
Transferring into clearer views.

Twenties, thirties into forties,
Time forever on your side.
Years to discover, ideas reborn,
Prospects good spirits high.

Progression of time,
Autumn has come.
Pace, becomes slower,
Reflect what's been accomplished.
Each moment to savour,
Infinite pride.

Lorna Kirby

THE ARMOURER

I well remember as a child in innocence and fun,
The sudden sombre interest found when looking at a gun.
A sight so rare in my young life, whatever is it for?
How sinister when it points at me with wide and gaping bore.

A quirk of fate then led me on when we found ourselves at war,
That caused me to spend many hours gazing through a bore.
For the hand of chance and service to the country that I love,
Had fostered greater interest and had given me a shove.

Towards a trade to follow for the rest of my sweet life,
'Well someone's got to do it' was the weak excuse to my dear wife.
'For firearms do not grow on trees to be plucked as they're desired,'
'They are so carefully manufactured and adjusted ere they're fired.'

We ply our business silently without announcement boast or fuss,
To support our comrade servicemen and their trust they put in us.
To keep them armed what ere the cost and to serve them in the field,
For we are soldiers also and (of course), would never yield.

For the ancient art of armoury by necessity must be done,
Although sinister in its purpose it involves us, everyone.
For man's first thought was for defence of all that he held dear,
Hence, sling-shot, bows and arrows, clubs and swords and hunting spear!

Charles J Hill

THE GOOD OLD DAYS

In days of old, in the past,
furniture and things were made to last,
not formica, chipboard or hardwood,
but real solid pine and oakwood.

Trams and trains on rails were run,
through valleys the only transport for some.
No more collieries which dug under the town,
subsidence, buildings have been pulled down.

Churches and chapels of which were many,
now there are few if any.
Sunday once was a day of rest,
nowadays shops open up and put to the test.

Since the day of thrupney bit and half a crown,
lots of things have changed in this town.
The pace was much slower, prices much lower,
Ah! Those were the days, they were the best.

Haydn Ashmead

LOOKING BACK

Paint and putty I could tell
Dad was home, this was his smell.
His work was on a building site
That smell I'd wait for every night.
Thursday evening pay day treats
I'd eagerly await for sweets.
Or sometimes to a picture show
Together dad and I would go.
Huddles around a roaring fire
Imaginations he'd inspire.
With stories of his childhood day,
And all the games he used to play.
Mum provided buttered toast,
While we sailed round the Ivory Coast.
As dad recalled his days at sea,
No-one took in more than me.
I'd hang on each and every word,
Tall stories like you've never heard.
A warm glow looking back I feel
Those childhood days which still appeal.

Barbara Entwistle

LIFE IN THE PAST

Many years ago when we were poor,
We were not afraid to answer the door.
To the person on the other side,
And be tempted to run away and hide.

A stranger was not our enemy, if
he spoke to us, while out at play.
We were not afraid, when he came to greet
and offer us a sweet.

When we were small we were not afraid at all,
Of the door to door salesman who
came to call.
They really were the people's friend
And on their goods you could depend.

We used to walk a mile to school
And didn't dare to play the fool.
The teachers then were very strict,
And not afraid to use a stick.

They say these were the good old days,
They were in many, many ways.
For when we're young, we have such fun,
And never count the cost.

Iris Covell

NO-MAN'S LAND

I have witnessed the giant steps that Man has made
In the universe,
Thrusting frenetically ever forward,
On his crusade
Into the supersonic age,
Without compassion.
Over all of nature riding roughshod,
Ousting the need for God.

Buffeted on the wind of change,
Balancing the past and the future
Uneasily, between the familiar 'old'
And the 'new' that is strange;
On the brink of the millennium,
I hover, uncertain
Of what the new century will bring,
Unhappily filled with foreboding.

B Gordon

A SIGN OF OUR TIMES

When she was asleep, they came one night,
Those cowardly, faceless thugs.
She was too frail to put up a fight,
And they were still high on drugs.
Her body's mended, but not her heart.
Her few possessions have gone.
They've torn her safe, peaceful home apart.
Do they care what they have done?
The tears have long ago ceased to flow,
Her eyes are lifeless and dull.
It's hard to believe, seeing her now,
She'd lived her life to the full.
Now she feels so utterly bereft,
Of all that she once held so dear.
Her memories are all she has left.
She views the future with fear.
Today she sits in a rocking chair,
Her independence has gone.
She's living under communal care,
At least she won't be alone.

Ann Lysons

BEFORE CARS

Only the doctors and vicars had cars, we had a pony and trap,
The donkey was old with only one eye, but could still go quite fast for all that.
He would trot down the lane, and we'd bounce up and down,
It would take us forever to get into town.
But we had all day so we didn't complain, but laughed and talked as we bowled down the lane,
People would call out 'Look out here comes old Ned' but he knew where to go without being led,
He would stop on the corner outside the old store, where he would get fed carrots galore.
Then he would sleep, he just wouldn't budge, though you pulled and tugged old Ned wouldn't budge.
But once he woke up would start with a clatter, making the women and children all scatter.
When he came to a hill, he would just stop, you had to get off till he got to the top.
Then once more you could climb back into the trap, and
Ned would start off without getting a slap.
He would trot all the way to the door of the shed, waiting with patience to go to his bed
Until the next time you would get the trap out, he would come trotting without having to shout
Ned might be old but is better than cars, for he can steer home by the light of the stars.

Winifred Jenkins

PARADISE ISLE

Fields are barren
Crops are rare.
Thieved by scavengers
The soldiers who dare.
Island beauty is
Suppressed by war.
Loved ones lost
Grief was raw.
But Jersey folk, resilient
Not weak.
Hidden caches of food
Treasures to seek.
Prisoners on paradise
For their heritage fight.
As fishing boats glide
Under cover of night.
Curfews ignored
Faith never dies.
Forbidden radios whisper
With news of allies.
Liberation was sweet
Freedom was near.
Learning to live again
Of life have no fear,
But many thoughts spared
For men never to come back.
To see the glory of Jersey
With its beauty, no lack.

Lorraine Pigrome

TIME TO REMEMBER

Wistful thoughts come to my mind . . .
. . . When I have time to ponder.
I drift back to the years gone by,
As though childhood times I wander.

Playing hopscotch in the street,
Or, swinging in the park.
Never a thought for danger . . .
. . . Not even after dark.

Sweets were such a special thing . . .
. . . For those who had been good.
We'd make them last a whole week long,
That's if we possibly could!

Blackjacks, peardrops, liquorice too . . .
. . . Gobstoppers that changed from
Red to blue.
These were the things that we liked best,
Always busy . . . no time to rest.

Today, when I sit and dream,
I wish I had a time machine.
To go back to those happy days . . .
. . . But, I still have my
memories, not just for now,
But always!

Pat Drew

WAY BACK WHEN

Do you remember when we were kids,
The games we played, the things we did
Knock down Ginger, whips and tops.
Skipping ropes and old hopscotch,
Sno-fruits and ice cream from a man on a trike.
(And we'd never heard of a mountain bike).
The milkman with his cart and horse,
And the man selling cockles and winkles of course.
A packet of crisps, with a blue salt bag.
('And don't get dirty,' mum would nag)
Saturday pictures for all of a penny,
(Take some sweets - if we had any)
Beano, Dandy and Film Fun too,
Trams, trolley buses and trips to the zoo.
Men mended roads with wood and tar,
(And we'd never heard of a 'Burger-Bar')
A penn'oth of chips in greasy paper,
(Not in a bag - 'cos that came later)
Black jacks, milk gums and big gob-stoppers -
That'd fill your mouth, 'cos they were whoppers.
Hot fresh bread, thick butter too.
And dripping toast we loved to chew.
Cough mixture and syrup of figs,
A Southend holiday in 'digs'.
The wireless gave us music, ITMA and Uncle Mac,
(Strange, it was always sunny, whenever we look back)
No computers, videos, CD's,
Or discos, stereos, TV's.
We made our own amusements then -
And enjoyed our lives too - way back when.

Janet B Boor

WAR

The air is still the sky is blue,
But don't let that be fooling you.
The air-raid siren sounds again,
And soon the deadly bombs will rain.
As the bombers drop their loads,
It seems as every street explodes.

All the people run around,
They know they must get underground.
To escape the catastrophe of death,
Little children hold their breath.
Mothers hold their loved ones near,
Trying to soothe in them, their fear.

The all-clear sounds and they slowly come out,
Rubble and bodies strewn about.
Muffled cries, shouts and moans,
From people buried beneath their homes.
All around is pain and sadness,
When will someone stop this madness.

The battlefields they must be cleared,
To finish off this war we feared.
Sons and fathers not coming home,
Mothers and children left alone.
All world leaders they should learn,
Wars like this should not return.

Heather Keeping

NOW AND THEN

How glad I am that I am old enough
To look with jaundiced eye upon the world
Today, and judge it far inferior
To that wherein I spent my happy youth.
Even the six long years of war did not
Confront us with such louring clouds of fears
That dim the pleasures of our present young
And blunt the keenness of their taste for life.
We ate whatever food we could obtain -
Good, wholesome fare -
No noxious pesticides,
No fears of sugar, starch or fat or additives,
To temper our enjoyment of our meals:
No thoughts of BSE or CJD
We smoked with nought to fear except a cough.
We'd never heard of AIDS or heroin,
Or pot or acid or amphetamines.
And glue was used for sticking things together!
The only struggles on the football field
Were those between the two opposing teams.
The terraces were safe - as were the streets
For folk to walk about, even at night.
We never thought of life without a job,
The future was our own and not controlled,
By politicians fingers poised to press
The fatal button - 'Tomorrow's cancelled!'
Oh yes! We lived in happier days than these,
And I am grateful that I was so blest.
I would not trade a single memory
To start again - the cost would be too great
To be a 1990's youth my fate.

Michael Hewlett

THOSE WERE THE DAYS

Can you remember when you were courting?
And still it was the fashion
Because it isn't today, they do anyway
When it comes to love and to passion.

Biggest thrill was at the pictures
Sitting on the back two rows.
They had special seats for courters,
They were double ones you know.

Some of the films had sub-titles,
So as you got the gist of the plot.
Trouble was if you couldn't read
Would you know who it was that got shot?

Some folk used to like Mae West
While others liked Charlie Chaplin best.
But if you wanted a gripping fright
You'd love to watch Pearl White.

The villain tied her to the railway line,
Usually in the pouring rain.
But the old lass usually managed to escape
By a whisker in front of the train.

Oh excitement wasn't to look for
By jove we were having fun.
But then we had to be home by half past nine,
When all was said and done.

The things we did when in our teens,
When we were young and full of beans.
Will always stay within our minds,
As memories of the better kind.

Anthony John Gibson

THE DAY MY DAD CAME HOME FROM SEA

In 1968 when I was ten
And my brothers were eight and three,
One Sunday morning I recall so well,
The day my dad came home from sea.

I wore my best dress and ponied my hair,
Mum let me wear lipstick and scent.
The boys were scrubbed and dressed up in their best,
For once I heard no argument.

Mum looked so pretty and happy that day.
For two years we had been apart.
And when dad finally stood at our front door,
I knew I loved him with all my heart.

He was in uniform, cap under arm,
And smiling all over his face.
He looked so handsome, so tall and so proud,
We rushed into his strong embrace.

While mum patiently waited for her turn,
Their eyes never left each other.
I will never forget how proud I felt,
To have my father and mother.

The best of my memories will always be
The day my dad came home from sea.

Shelley Jones

THE MEGABYTES OF THE ROUND TABLE

A massive metal mega-droid
Created in some lab-like void.
By a professor with a strange desire
To see a world engulfed in fire.

'A world stands aflame; Aglow.'

And as he hailed his new creation,
A priest *'Doom'* prophesied,
The masses soon drugged to elation
In worship. It's suicide!

'The Anti-Christ, a devil's here
With flaming sword and wounding spear'

Yet, like baked dough with a hint of yeast,
An army grew; A great uprising,
For the Feast
So appetising.

'Far away hum'

A ritual unveiling soon took place,
Yet no one stopped to mourn,
But hailed the thing from 'outer space'
As a Knight-like Beast was born.

'Hear the loud drum'

This creature built for 'Your Defence'
'As a Deterrent for the Foe'!
Amid the game-plans, cold yet dense,
And a world aflame; Aglow.

'Hear as they, watch as they, fear as they come'

A massive metal mega-droid,
Created in some lab-like-void,
A 'Super-human' A 'Super-mind'
That came and wiped out humankind.

Andrew Grundy

THE PUNK

He suddenly appeared before me one day
Like an apparition from some weird alien place
With hair resembling spiked pink candy-floss
And legs clad in red plaid
Bound about with cord and strap.
The thing-ummy dangling from the back
I later learned was called a bum-flap!
His shirt was torn, and on it written and drawn
In black were swastikas
And words like Anarchy! And Long Live Sid!
An abundance of safety-pins were everywhere
About his person, including one through an ear.
And oh heck! A studded dog collar
Complete with padlock encircled his neck.
'Who are you! What are you! Why do you dress
Like that?' I asked, wanting to understand
He answered 'Because I'm a punk and I'm in a band
This is our gear. We like to be different that's all.'
'But you and your friends,' I said 'all look alike.'
'So what! I'm not listening,' he replied
'I'm a punk mum and that's that.'

Patricia Millicent Hanson

CAVEAT

Maintain no links with our nations,
This festering, cancerous body - civilisation,
No decadence, nor corruption, no senseless crime,
Nothing resembling mankind serving time.

No disease, no squalor, certainly no strife.
Everything is valued, including life.
Our ship, civilisation, takes an unscheduled ride,
Lacking, uncertain, on a variable tide.

Learn from the rat race gnawing at its own foundations
Too late we realised the serious implications.
A species that destroys that on which it relies,
Nature . . . the land, sea and the skies.

Too late we value what cannot be regained.
The various species ignorantly strained.
Lo, behold the dregs are alive,
Mankind, ironically, adapts to survive.

What you have protect and cherish,
Safeguard nature, watch her flourish,
Remember the fate awaiting civilisation,
Never breathe the air of desolation.

Our cancer could grow, swell out of proportion,
Pray for immunity, proceed with caution.
Be like a mouse, avoiding a cat
Caveat! Heed the experienced voice of a rat.

Mandy Sowerby

IN RETROSPECT

I start to bend and, slow of gait,
Am stigmatised as *elderly,*
But those like me may mediate,
Fragments of sweet, pale pictures see.
No paintings ticketed *For Sale,*
No revolutionised technique,
No golden image nor grisaille,
For me past precious colours speak.
Our world, tormented, fast rotates,
Casting my thoughts - as bridal train -
To slither whilst a future waits
And sometimes saddened tears remain.
Yet I alone have a private view;
Humour my quiet as tired, I walk.
Re-living moments once I knew;
Nodding, I find no need to talk.
My gem stones in a store-house gleam,
Jewels of peace, treasures of trust.
Unique experience in dream
Shall hardly tarnish, fail to rust.
You may not notice when I pause,
Bewildered by the present noise,
Fragile maybe, but I have cause
To court approaching time when joys
Clear, unadulterated - great -
Shut out the sudden, fearful day.
Life moves on - it's getting late
But memory honeys the way.

Ruth Daviat

THE PERFECT DAY

As morning brings, the icy frost,
Nature's left all cold and moist,
The sun which gives a bright, warm glow,
Creeps up the meadows, as they grow.
Trickles of water, which lead to a stream,
Sunshine reflects, a glistening beam,
Rabbits run freely, from burrow to burrow,
Making their acquaintance, to each other.
As night time brings, the cool, blue breeze,
The moon shines through the rustling trees,
The swoop of an owl, which kills its prey,
Ends another, perfect day.

Charlotte Cocker

BACK TO THE FUTURE

Study the past to manage the present
and to have hope for the future
by learning, try not to resent
The sad mistakes we must endure
for on the day we cannot see
results right for *our* age
we do not always hold the key,
or have the hindsight of a Mage.
Time travel to past and future
would surely aid us in our quest.
But that is a forbidden cure,
maybe to stay in our own time is best.

Ivy Allpress

NOSTALGIA

How many of us keep I wonder
Childhood toys of days gone by?
Spinning tops, and broken hoops
in the attic, where they lie
tatty and mostly quite forgotten,
never, see the light of day
Then the Vicar calls, 'Some jumble,
anything will do - OK?'
So we look into the attic
where we spend an hour or two
Can we part with any jumble?
No! This is where our dreams came true!
One eyed dolls, faded soldiers
became our comrades-in-arms
fighting valiantly together
we won our battles - all false alarms!
What's in this box, I wonder
then I gaze in sheer delight
Glowing marbles, big and small ones
I sit and play till daylight's out of sight.
Goodness gracious, is that the time?
The family will be home for tea
A last look round, a happy sigh
Ah, what else do I see?
I can't believe at last I've found him
Many years I've looked here and there
Did he think that I'd forgotten?
No, he's still my precious *Teddy Bear!*

Edna G Trickey

REFLECTION OF LIFE

How very strange life seems to be
Is that mirror reflection, really me,
I remember when I was young
My body straight and very strong.

I look at my hair, it has turned grey
Not quite as thick as yesterday.
Some people say it looks alright
But soon my hair will turn to white.

Distinctive lines upon the face
Life's problems are there for all to trace
My body looks a different shape
Old age creeps up, there's no escape.

But in the mirror what do I see
This strange reflection that's looking at me.
Contentment and happiness most of his life
A very nice family, and a jolly good wife.

Dennis N Davies

WIMBLEDON JACK

My first love was a chap called Jack
Who hung out daily on the hill
Immaculately attired, brass buckles, black,
He gave the giggling girls a thrill.

Jack was a big well muscled fellow
Who always drew admiring glances,
I once went up and said 'Hello,'
But he tossed his head at my advances.

Jack helped the tired, large and small,
I have a postcard of him still,
A gentle giant who pulled for all
This magnificent trace horse on the hill.

I doubt there are many left alive
Who remember Jack in his painted box
Enjoying a quiet nosebag snack. In '25
He was retired: my love was lost.

Jean Mitchell

FIFTIES CHILD

Flags of stone
Horse and cart;
Rag and bone,
Roller skates
Cobbled streets
Childhood mates.
Hoola hoops
Kick and run,
Chicken coops
Coconut or goldfish
Saturday morning flicks
Those little golden birdies
A secret wish,
Winkle picker shoes;
Short, back and sides, brylcream,
Baggie long pant blues,
Little girls
Mystery's dream

N Bannister

REMEMBERING

Oh! Stondon is my birthplace,
And Stondon is my home.
It's where I've lived for years and years
With no desire to roam.
A village small with country lanes
Green meadows, country walks,
A sparkling brook, a tiny church,
A place where nature talks.

Contented cows and friendly horses,
Song of birds, the church bell ringing,
Sunday morning, peace abounding
A summer's day is just beginning.
The scent from hedgerows fills the air
The golden corn is everywhere.
Pigs are grunting, ducks a-quacking,
And we've the time *to stand and stare.*

This my dream of long ago.
And who shall say me nay?
When memory speaks of times long past.
To the greatly changed world of today.

But that was then and this is now,
Gone are those days I knew.
Those days of sweet tranquillity
Remembered only by the few;
Time marches on relentlessly
And life takes on a different view,
The scene has changed for you and me,
Do not forget what used to be.

Edith Gaskin

WHEN I WAS YOUNG

When I was young, the sun shone all day, every day.
I know that because, we never missed our going out to play.
Sometimes in the summer, a thunderstorm would come.
But, the sun would soon shine warm again, when, the rain was gone.

When I was young, girls had long hair, with pigtails and bows.
They wore button boots and, pinafores over their clothes.
If boys were about, they would giggle and, laugh with each other.
And, they'd dress and undress dolls and, pretend to be mother.

When I was young, we would play marbles, bowl hoops and, whip tops.
And, leap frog and throw stones at the church tower clocks.
We knew all the birds' nests, for many miles around.
And, we always knew where the first apples had fallen on the ground.

When I was young, it was quite safe to go out.
And, any woman could go anywhere without
Fear of molestation and, wrongdoers were caught.
And, until they left school, all small boys wore shorts.

When I was young, old people were held in respect.
And, they could tell of things which, held our interest.
They knew so many things which, we always wanted to know.
And they would smile and say yes but, first you must grow.

When I was young, I'm sure the world was a much nicer place.
It's all hurry now and, everything done at such a great pace.
We gave time to each other then but, things still got done.
In that dear dead, old fashioned past when, I was young.

George Harcourt

PARALIEL

The past is over, gone
We must learn to let go
For, no matter what
We cannot have it back
And this is rightly so.

The future, is yet to come
The unknown
Mingled with joy and sadness
Good, along with a darker force
For this is our universal law

The present, is now
That, which we bear responsibility for
You and I, my friend have
The key in our hands
For this - our present time

Therefore The Past, Present and Future
Are all linked,
And cannot be disentangled.

Irene Gunnion

NEIGHBOURS

Why were neighbours, long ago,
        More friendlier, than today,
Was it because, they were mostly your relatives,
        Who kept, in touch, each day?

But now, if you're ill, and needing help,
        Your neighbours, don't seem to care,
Yet years ago, when they made a meal,
        They'd bring you, in a share.

And if your children, misbehaved,
As youngsters, always do,
Your neighbours, would chastise them,
And then report, to you.

But now, people don't seem to take the time,
To stop, and chat, anymore,
So you're very lucky nowadays,
If you know the folk next door.

Jean Hendrie

HOW MANY?

How many eyes have gazed out
through that dirty window pane
How many lives have paused to view
How many empty shadows can
the walls recall to mind
How many sighs were heaved
like mine while missing you.

How many lovers tussled
just above these creaking boards
How many babies cried at night
How many youngsters clattered
up and down the narrow stairs
How many lonely souls who
wished they'd got it right.

How many sheets have hung out
on that back-yard washing line
How many bags of coal were bought
How many flowers have been
picked and handed on to friends
How often in the darkness
clung to solace sought.

Andrew Hodson

20TH CENTURY MILESTONES

The telephone is a utility, the computer a must.
The dishwasher, dryer with a-many programmes,
Like aeroplane consoles inside our homes.
Instead of: 'I'll drop you a few lines.'
Now it's: 'I'll fax you.'

Children's minds have collectively forgotten,
Hopscotch, catch and hide and seek.
Baa baa black sheep's out of fashion
And chairperson's on the way in.
There is Save the Whales,
Save the Dolphins.
The ozone layer is deplete.
There is Greenpeace,
Rain forests on the decrease.

Forrest Gump has made big news
Pushing Bosnia to the side.
Jehovah Witnesses' date of doom has come and gone,
The war to end all wars is history,
The war that put *holocaust* in dictionaries is past.
Russia is no longer USSR
The Iron Curtain, Berlin Wall are felled.
America is in debt.
Japan and Germany masters once again.

The years keep rolling by,
'94, '95, '96
A necklace of pearls and lead
Chokes modern us.
The year two thousand looms so close at hand.
Are we prepared?

Mariella Cassar

1896

A little girl skipped happily along the dusty road,
Her intention was to visit a good friend.
She knew she was forbidden to go outside the gate,
This was a rule that she would often bend.
Though her trip she knew full well would incur her mother's wrath
The fascination that it held was far too strong
For 'Old Moore' told many stories that held her quite enthralled
Although she knew that she was doing wrong.
'One day when you're a woman grown, you'll stand out in this road,
Wondering where the horses have all gone
For men and women both will ride in horseless carriages
Rose, mark my words, you'll see that I'm not wrong.'
Rosanna's eyes shone brightly as she thought of things to come
And could hardly wait to see if he was right
The thought of horseless carriages was such a wild idea
She would lie awake and think of them at night.
He said that men would one day sit in the bellies of silver birds
And fly around above her in the sky
'I know folk say I'm mad Rose, but I'm sure it won't be long 'til
The quickest way to travel is to fly.'
He said that in her lifetime she would own a great machine
To do the family washing by itself
No dolly-tub or mangle or wooden scrubbing board
Sitting in the wash-house on a shelf.
Rosanna was my grandmother, she loved that dear old man
And for years she recalled his every word
She learned to drive, her car came first, then her washing machine
But best of all she flew in her silver bird

Daphne Thomas

THE PAST TO ME

Elegant ladies in fine pure dresses,
Elegant men in fine smart suits,
Their manners so perfect and
    right.

The elegant ladies feel like
    a lady,
The elegant men are fine proper
    brought-up gentlemen.

The children running in the streets,
    with their marbles and
    their conkers,
The little girls with pretty
    ribbons in their hair,
    and their golden curls.
The little boys with caps,
    and their short brown hair.

The streets so friendly,
People so willing to help,
    the world so warm and
    loving and tender.

The past so pure and
    so free,
That's the past
    to me.

Lee-anne Goodhead

YESTERDAY

(So long ago when I was twelve)

In my class at my school, we had a dunce's desk
And I sat there for half a term, because I was a pest.

You can't believe it can you Ben! (My son aged twelve.)
That your dear mum was bad.
But I could be quite awful and I made my teacher mad.

In fact she really liked me - we did get on quite well
It was just now and then I had a mad and stupid spell.

You kids don't know (I'm sad to say)
What Beatlemania be, but I contracted it quite bad in 1963.

It was a generation bug - that we all seemed to get
You had to have this Beat-all-thing, to be in the In Set

So that first year in Secondary School, I did not learn a thing.
Except about those Liverpool lads, and how well they could sing.

It did effect my school work, yeah yeah I know it's bad.
My books were covered with their names, I was quite Beatle mad.

Always away in dreamland, whenever they rang the bell.
The only thing I could talk about, the only word that I could spell.

In maths only the famous 4, was entered in my book
In PE it was twist and shout until the teacher shook (with rage.)

But every scrap of info, about those four sunk in
My attention knew no boundaries, my brain full to the brim.

My teacher didn't know these lads, knowledge there she lacked.
But by the end of that school term, I'd taught her every fact.

I thought it really was the *ticket,* I think she got a rough *ride.*
But when the end of term approached, my teacher sat and cried.

Don't think she'd ever forget me though, she mainly kept her cool.
But I often think *those were the days,* when I was still at school.

Frances Rapley

THOSE QUIETER DAYS

I remember the days when time
seemed to stand still.
We worked hard in our work
and at play.
There wasn't the madness of
rushing around.
You gave people the time of day.

Spring was the season that felt
so full of life
Summers were all sunny and dry.
Fresh air really was fresh air
With a clear blue blanket of sky.

Folk cycled for miles over dusty
old roads.
Nature was in charge of us then.
Meadows and hedges, the sounds
of the birds.
God's garden meant peace to
all men.

Raymond Powell

BLACK IS THE COLOUR

Black are the hearts of men of evil
They who care not who they maim.
Black is the hatred of the men of Satan
Death is the name of their gruesome game.

Black is the future for Northern Ireland
If these terrorists are to remain.
Black is the fear we fight to conquer
As once more they fight to reign.

Black were the nights we knew in London
During the war hearing the planes.
Black was our despair then
But never was our spirit broken.

And never will it again.

Lydia E Stanton

DUNNOTAR CASTLE

The sweetest perfume of horse-breath,
Hustle-bustle of seagull-studded cliffs,
Solitary seal caressing coolmint waters.
I was there and inhaled such completeness.

Stairs shiny under lithe-footed traffic,
Vast ovens exhaling warm, moist breath,
Heavy with the scent of bread and beef and salt.

Stumbling into pot-bellied vaults
Where awkward captives crouch,
Slinking in and out of earthy corridors,
Blind as a worm.

Into the drawing room, belittled by awe,
Surveying the suicide precipice,
Crested waves tumbling.

Then the chapel, magnificently discreet,
Touching gritty stones; connecting with my ancestors,
Filled with electric-shock revelation.
This is history and I am here,
So connected, time does not exist.
I drop a penny in the well
And hear the voices of my kinspeople.

Kirstie Munro-Jelks

THE PAST DOWN ON THE FARM

The past is heavy horses slowly plodding round the fields
Turning soil and sowing seeds trying to give a better yield
Nothing enclosing either man nor beast as a stormy weather shield
From dawn till dusk, mile after mile on a solitary meal
Those days are gone

The past is following a binder cutting corn at harvest time
Stacking sheaves to dry them out in long and perfect lines
Then build high and true on horse carts - which was a proper craftsman's sign
Then the sweat and graft at threshing time was for those only in their prime
Those days are gone

The cattle tied in steamy sheds standing quietly day after day
Fed and mucked by barrow as it was the only way
Milked by hand, then into cans round to the loading bay
Or carried to another shed where the calves all used to stay
Those days are gone

The past is struggling up into the lost with heavy corn filled sacks
Which meant aching arm and shoulders and a lifetime pain in backs
Once there they were not finished as they'd to be built in two high stacks
Only the strong and fittest ever seemed to have the knack
Those days are gone

The past is filling carts by hand with turnips in the bitter cold first light
Up and down the frosted drills until it was filled up right
Hands and feet still numb and tingling when the dark comes down at night
When a blazing fire and steaming soup was by far the most longed for sight
These days are gone

The past is six big strapping farmhands when now one is all they need
For tending to the livestock for their bedding and their feeds
He'll also manage all the landwork from plough to the sowing of the seeds
With increasing farming companies buying all the family farmers' deeds
The old days are gone

Christopher Leith

STAR QUESTERS

I send you greetings from the empty stars . . .
Now we have reached the glorious galaxy's brink
We are cold in living graves
No longer feeling, lost in joy or grief,
But merely made to think.
This giant ship in whose hard shell I work,
I eat, I breath, I count the years and sleep
Had been marked and cracked,
Like me,
By countless miles . . .
And only in my dreams I weep.
My eyes are dry,
Have long lost wonder for
The Universal Soul,
I only know a vast eternal nothing
Is my goal.

I send you greetings from the empty stars . . .
There is a cruelty in no joy, no pain, no fear.
Do not follow us,
But keep your loves, your wars,
Your scant mortality,
And hold them dear.
For us, condemned by science to
The everlasting void,
There are no smiles,
No gentle touch that warms the night . . .
And harder still . . . no tears.

Kris Dickson

THE FARM LABOURER'S LOT

The *Good Old Days* we're often told,
Were those which were the best:
But best for whom? (I ask myself)
The rich - but what about the rest?

Working long hours, with a mean wage to boot;
Families large, with not enough to eat.
No time for leisure, life constant toil -
Food bread, cheese, onions - but seldom meat.

Out in all weathers, sacks wrapped around legs;
Army boots from war-days worn upon feet.
Winter start at the first light of dawn,
And summer long hours in harvest-time heat

Often until the sun sank down to rest,
(Perhaps also shaking with sweat and fatigue?)
Returning weary, home mean without comfort;
Head under pump, supper always meagre.

Lungs exhausted, with heart and head thudding;
Knowing the sun would soon pierce him like knife;
Lying with wife early-aged through child-bearing,
No hope of improvement, life unchanging strife.

Ailments frequently went unheeded;
Trust in God was all *he* could afford!
Neglect could sometimes lead him to sorrow,
An early return to sod and the Lord.

Wondering sometimes about life's good things,
Reality soon had its sway. Why, the hymn said:
'Each one to his Estate' - so he *should* know
That fortune always must pass *him* by!

Thy will, not mine, Lord!

Elizabeth Elsie Lovell

INSOUCIANT

Last night I walked down Memory Lane,
I thought I'd see you there.
The memories all came flooding back
Of times we used to share.
Of hanging round the coffee bars
In plastic knee length boots,
Our back combed, bouffant, bleach blond hair,
Much darker at the roots.
Frothy coffee, smoke filled rooms
And teddy boys in leather,
We'd rock around the clock all night,
And double date together.
We'd black our eyes, panstick our cheeks
And brightly paint our lips.
We'd copy Twiggy, Mary Quant,
With skirts that reached our hips.
We'd jive beneath fluorescent lights,
Dancing to the latest,
You liked Elvis, I liked Cliff -
The Beatles were the greatest.
We hung around with boys on bikes,
The smell of oil and grease.
Guitars strumming, smoking pot,
And greeting all with 'peace.'
We banned the bomb and burnt our bras,
Wore flowers in our hair.
Last night I walked down Memory Lane
I thought I'd see you there.

Diane Rees

ATLANTIS

The oceans are vast and horizons far
Once navigated by sun and star,
Untold mysteries lie beneath the depths
Strange fish, treasure and shipwrecks.

What great lands are there to be found
Once great nations the waters did pound,
Into oblivion no more to be seen
Lands with mountains, rivers and everything green.

Were these lands the lands of the Gods
Who shot thunderbolts from magic rods,
Whom man toiled for in ages past
In an age which was not to last.

The Gods returned to starry space
Never to return to that wondrous place,
When the waters came the people fled
Kings were left on Earth to rule instead.

They fled in boats to other lands
Others perished in their thousands,
Beneath the oceans raging masses
This land lies which was called Atlantis.

David G Smith

TEENAGE YEARS

Tantrums and tears and endless fears,
And this is it . . . the teenage years!

Spots and rashes and endless dashes,
To here and there and everywhere.

Talking on the 'phone for hours and hours
Staying out late, feeling so tired.

Insolence and gloom, sadness and doom,
Everyone saying, she'll grow out of it soon.

Deceit and defiance, secret alliance,
Screaming and shouting, this is doing my head in!

Oh how I caused them, problems a plenty,
Now I can see it! Now that I'm twenty!

Maureen Cunningham

OH FOR DAYS PAST

People helped each other
They lived their lives as one
No expensive toys for us
We made our own kind of fun

Clothing coupons ration books
No decent shoes upon our feet
Life was oh so different in those bygone days
People worked so hard just to make ends meet

The old mangle standing in the yard
Buckets of blue to soak the whites
Monday was washday
Whether it be dull or bright

Home made bread and cakes
For Sunday was the day they baked
We all went to Sunday school clothes all neatly pressed
I always felt special dressed in my Sunday best.

Life today is not the same
It's all hifi, video and computer games
TV killed conversation nobody wants to chat
Oh how I would love to see the old days back

Gillian Morrisey

HE HAS GONE

I can remember
How one or two
Elderly folk
Respectfully took off their hats
As the hearse in procession
Drove by.

Lou would have remarked on that;
He was of that age.
He was of that time
When folk would always do that sort of thing;
You know - being thoughtful-like,
Having a respect for the dead
And for the mourners too!

Lou was like that.
It was what he would have done.

Yes, that was Lou -
He was respectful.
He had thought for others.
He would have raised his hat too.

But alas he has gone -
And his like is passing.

L Simcock-Daisy

SUSPENDED IN THE FOURTH DIMENSION

. . . Therefore the universe has no ending;
Volumeless, without boundaries, is space
Which the depth of planets is borrowing;
Orbiting that area like a face
In a mirror: filling the lonely void,
Rippling at places where the heat has cloyed

Like bubbles in heated sand - vast desert
Hanging on the wall, many faceted,
Catching the echoes of images - pert
Prisms which reflected and diverted
Light. Dropping the mirror won't shatter the clime;
The spilled liquid is drowned by pervasion of space.
Though debris clutters it, makes too heavy for time;
Too tired, time whistles in the wind: end of the race!

Suzanne Stratful

LIFE'S END

The day I lost you, I wanted to die,
I looked down at your grave and wondered, why?
So full of life you always were
Why wasn't it me? I'll never be sure.
And as I stood there with tears in my eyes
Friends kissed my cheeks and said their goodbyes,
A cold wind was blowing and it started to rain
But all I felt was heartache and pain.
The sky grew dark, it was time to leave,
Everyone's gone, I'm alone to grieve.
A wonderful husband, and loyal friend
Through your whole life right to the end.
You loved and cared, and did your best,
Not just for me, but for all the rest.
So many flowers, so many friends,
Will it be the same at my day's end?
The pain has gone, but the ache's still there,
Sometimes it's almost too much to bare.
I've so many memories, this is true
But oh my love I wish I had you.
And as I stand by your grave in the rain,
I know in my heart, we will meet again.

Paddy Flatt

THE RUSH HOUR

Fingers tapping on the steering wheel
Surrounded by my symbol of steel
The spark plugs burn the Arabs earn
And I moved forward just one turn

The pretty girl standing at the bus stop
Receiving appraisal from the manly lot
Suddenly finds the desire
To read the time-table though it has expired

Rain goes plip plop on the screen
Just sufficient to make it unclean
A cyclist passes on the near side
Surely a form of suicide

Reach the roundabout at last
Revving up as if at Brands Hatch
Clutch out off we go
Cut up by a GTO

Control my temper as well as I can
Thinks have we a branch in the Isle of Man

Alan Clough

THE HILLS IN THE WINDOW

The snow lies in valleys, white ribs against dykes
The rest of it has crashed away eastwards,
The talk of wide rivers. Now the road is glassy,
Potholed with great pools; my feet are drunk
On sunken ledges of ice.

The farm has not changed.
Its Christmas windows welcomed me
When I was two feet smaller.
The grandaughter of the first collie I knew
Bounces out to meet me, a flow of black and white.

We are all of us older
But the hands are no less warm,
The friendship and talk as rich
As precious as in the beginning -
The hills in the window will always remain.

Kenneth Steven

HOPE

Bombs.
Blitz.
Destruction.
Rubble.
Despair. But hope
That good would triumph over evil.

Peace.
Wounded men.
Broken homes.
Repairs.
Rebuilding. New hope
That the future would be better.

Unemployment.
Overcrowding.
Drugs.
Old age.
Poverty. Still hope
That all will be right in time.

Health.
Happiness.
Friendship.
Love.
Sufficient wealth for our needs.
Hopes are fulfilled.

Wendy Richardson

MAN

The day of a caveman I wonder how it was
Rising up with the sun in a world that is new
And hunting animals with crude hand made spears
Creeping through forests that have yet to be cleared
Dressed only in skins and fur from his prey
I wonder if he was out hunting most of the day
Finding berries and fruit all along his path
Weaving through the forests he'll quickly go
To the cool clean river where he'll stop for a drink
No-one knows how to pollute it yet
The warm sun above is heating the land
And new life is still evolving all around man
The mountains are moving a spectacular sight
As a volcano erupts and gives man a fright
He somehow knows that the rivers of fire will not reach
Where he is standing surveying the scene
So man turns his back and stalks away in search of his prey
At last man sniffs the air the scent he has found
And he creeps along hidden by the tall green grass
Man has found animal he'll have dinner at last
He brings back his arm his spear has gone
Whistling through the air and into his prey
High above the sun is getting low in the sky
With his kill on his back man trudges home
Back over the river and through the forest to his cave
Where he will make the fire that he has learnt
And cook fresh meat for his supper tonight.

Christine Spurrell

MEMORIES

The wind blows cold against the window pane
washing water is frozen in the bowl again.
We cuddle up together in bed to keep warm
listening to the noises of the threatening storm.

Tiny mice feet patter around the bedroom
mingled with attic rats under the light of the moon.
We huddle up closer three in a bed
blankets pulled tight over our heads.

We awaken to daylight and frozen air
under blankets dressing our clothes to wear.
The lino feels cold beneath our feet
ice cold water. Frosted windows. No heat.

Long woolly socks lace up shoes
off to school not a moment to lose.
Braving the cold we make our way
over the same route everyday.

Stalling for time lingering about
knowing for certain we each get a clout.
Coal buckets to fill wood to be chopped
chickens to feed floors to be mopped.

Water to boil buckets to lug
into the parlour tipped into the tub.
Saturday bathtime one at a time
the youngest first as we stand in line.

O to be young again. Not for me
it wasn't so wonderful as it's made out to be.
The comforts and pleasures we have today
you can forget the past. Put it away.

Mary Moon Cole

MAYPOLE AT ELSTOW 1957-1958

A row of cottages in Shakespeare style, overhanging upper rooms
Bunting clad. Union Jacks, jutting from windows that looked out
Across the village green, where soon would be the Maypole scene

There Annie Berrick stood at her door, to welcome her friend
With her wrinkled smile. Down a step into her parlour, a cosy space,
Flowery curtains, cushions and antimacassars trimmed with lace.

Through in the next room such a spread of cakes, trifles, sandwiches
With home-made bread. In the centre a large fruit cake had to be,
'Twas made by Annie for this special tea.

Before the feast, a procession, with music and shuffle of feet,
Told us of its coming. We all rushed outside, except Baby Boy
Who was fast asleep, while his sister pushed through the crowd,
To get first peep at the white dresses and sashes. Boys looking
Smart, bashful, grinning, marching to keep pace with the cart
And band, in their white laced plimsolls all looking grand.

Cart all covered with paper flowers, created by small hands
Over many hours. Men in the shafts as the load was light,
Three young maidens, one to be Queen. Decorated wheels rolled
Through the wide gate, paper garlands arched overhead as girls,
Boys in all directions fled, to sit on grass to wait for the dancing.
Town crier in his red coat, with top hat, no taller than the gate post
He had passed, reached the platform at last to make his speech.

The Queen of May now seated on her throne, he made his announcement
Of her crowning, loudly with aid of microphone.
Then over loud speakers a chord is struck, suddenly the high pole
Jerks, then rocks, as maidens in flouncing frocks, white shoes and socks,
Together with lads on their best behaviour, weave neat patterns
With ribbons intertwined. Then back to Annie Berrick, there to find
The party in full swing, we talk and sing a wonderful *May Day.*

Dorothy French

A FRESH START

I know it's time, I have to go,
other places, new people to get to know.

Holidays, weekends, I will be here,
but the rest of my life I shall be elsewhere.

I'm scared to death, I'm living proof,
I haven't a life and that's the truth.

If I face the facts then I'll be fine,
I'll do any job, get away from the unemployment line.

I'll miss my family and my friends,
It will be a fresh start, on myself I shall depend.

Sitting at the table writing this letter,
It may cheer me up, may even make me feel better.

I know I have to do it, stand on my own two feet,
perhaps then my life will be more complete.

I could tell my story of when I was a child,
and think of the days of when I ran wild.

To never feel the love of a mother or father,
so what the hell, what's all the palaver.

Yes it's time, on my own two feet I shall stand,
then all my rights I shall demand.

Prove them all wrong and that's what I'll do,
so thanks a lot gran, it's all down to you.

You've both helped me through the good and the bad,
and been to me like a mum and a dad.

And I'll wait for the day when you say out loud,
that your granddaughter has done you really proud.

S Priestley

THE OLD PITS

If the whistle between shifts blew
something was wrong the families knew.
They all ran to the pit head
between them hardly a word was said.

Children ran crying with their mams
the little bairns were in their prams.
Women with shawls around shoulder tight
each one praying with all their might.

Around in a tight cluster they all stood
hoping against hope the news would be good.
Lips trembling and eyes very wide
they all stood side by side.

From out of the shafts some men they came
all were blackened some were lame.
Blood was pouring from one head
against the coal dust it looked so red.

The men walked out so silently
daylight they were pleased to see.
With their families they walked homeward bound
all this was done without a sound.

Some families were left standing there
knowing the truth was hard to bare.
Silent tears flowed from their eyes
to their men there would be no goodbyes.

There had been an explosion underground
six men could not be found.
What had happened no-one knew
but missing was a six man crew.

Helen Simpson

LENHAM 1945

An aircraft growled in the distant sky -
Far away blue, summer gone by.
Insects hummed in green Church Meadow
When I was there those years ago.
Swirl in the road of dusty eddy,
Bees drowsed in lavender, scented heady,
Woodshed's dusty smell. The newspaper bore
Reports to read from the First World War.
In dug-out, clammy, cold
Lay damply, apples green and gold.
Eggs in water glass in the larder,
Dunkirk chocolate, saved, gets harder.
Top shelf, parkin, gingery browned,
Oatmeal, treacle, taste renowned.
Doodlebugs dreaded horrid sound,
Bars of my cot all around.
VE Day, chick in Lenham Square,
First prize in pram - just aware.
Rapid clackk of the parquet floor,
Curtain hanging from the door.
Through branches of the copper beech
Late sunlight flickered. Please could each
Moment of that summer dusk
With scented roses, moths and musk
Come alive and Lenham stay
The same today.

C Pearson

I REMEMBER . . .

I remember cold stone floors,
Dolly tubs and draughty doors,
Dolly pegs and aching legs,
Backs a-breaking, hernias making.
Turning, twisting - chilblains itching,
Washday in the farmhouse kitchen,
Great improvement now we're electric,
Washer with spinner, all automatic.

Black-leading the grate - not a romantic job,
Burning one's fingers on a really hot hob.
Black on your hands, black on your face,
Much better now there's no fireplace -
Turn on the gas, it's warm straight away,
No stoking and poking and cleaning all day.

There were no trams or traffic jams,
Just shanks' pony and a bike -
An ordinary bike - not the mountain type.
Now we have a Renault car,
More expensive, but better by far.

Picking wild flowers, out in the fields.
Bitten by bugs - covered in weals,
Itching and scratching, sneezing and wheezing,
Greenhouse flowers are just as pleasing.
Yes, we were happy with our lot
For truth to tell that's all we'd got.

It's not times past we hanker after,
But lost childhood, freedom and laughter.
Life never was all 'Mills and Boon' -
Gone, alas, was our youth, too soon.

J Weatherall

THOSE DAYS LONG AGO

My mind wanders back to those days long ago,
through the end of my shoe you could see my big toe.

The seat of my pants, there was always a hole,
my mam she would yell and often would scold.

Dad would get drunk most nights of the week,
and he'd give us a penny for some little treat.

His Sunday best suit mam would often pawn,
to buy a pig's head to make pressed brawn.

Off to the market mam would take me and you,
to buy us shoes, second hand, never new.

Perhaps next week a second hand dress,
but only to wear for our Sunday best.

The rent man would knock, I'd say mam's not in,
as she hid behind the door in our tiny kitchen.

All the kids on our street were a snotty nosed lot,
wiping their nose on their sleeve, 'cos no hanky they'd got.

No muggings, no rape, no lager louts
a box round the tab if you got found out.

Yes, those were the days, the best of my life,
no matter what happens, you can't wipe them out.

C Bearder

I REMEMBER MISS MOLE

Yes, I remember the name,
referred to in conversations
which ended at my approach.

The weather was of the kind
one always wishes
on a Sunday summer afternoon.
My father said:
'We are going to tea with Miss Mole.'

Carefully dressed, I recall
climbing a tree-lined hill,
descending stone steps,
then being seated in polite comfort
in a cool and shaded room.

I did not know what a mole was like
but this Miss Mole was rounded and rested;
one felt she did not have to struggle
to make ends meet.
She wooed us with tea and cake.

The room seemed charged
with my unchildlike anxiety,
my mother's veiled animosity,
my father's careful jollity
and Miss Mole's savoured moment of victory.

We visited once again
but it was not a success.
Her name was sometimes spoken
by edged voices,
then less often,
then no more.

Strange, that I should remember Miss Mole.

Louise Rogers

BACK TO THE FUTURE

'Higher, higher, touch the sky!', cries Nina merrily rushing by
Her arms outstretched, embracing the day, giggling and singing the clouds away
She runs up to me reaching out, and takes me by the hand, skipping along so happily, leaving footprints in the sand
I can feel her little fingers wrapped round mine tight, chattering so sweetly with sheer excitement and delight.

She's running round in circles, trailing a big stick in her hand, concentrating hard, drawing pictures of her Dad there in the sand
How shocked he would be if he could see his portrait, for his ears have grown somewhat, and he's put on lots of weight!
How I love these special moments, with just Nina and me, stroking the horses, playing games and paddling in the sea
These memories are ours, and I'm never letting go, how I love my darling daughter, more than she will ever know.

She says that Papa's a Power Ranger, and that he plays football, when the old guy's nearly sixty, with no energy at all -
To keep up with Nina, running in circles on the sand, he'd rather walk alongside us, with her holding tight to his hand
To her, Papa is immortal, her parents are not too bad, her sister is her play mate, the best friend she's ever had
She has her life before her, and now, so much to learn, but what ever happens to her, her needs I'll never spurn.

Now it's time for bed for Nina, the sandman's already been, I love to see her sleeping, so peaceful and serene
For the three years that we've had her, I've known how lucky we are, to be blessed with lovely daughters, and, of course, dear Papa.
In a way I dread to see her, grow up and touch the sky, because then she'll be a woman, and the years will pass me by
But I'll always have the memories of Nina running on the sand, and I'll still feel her little fingers, wrapped tightly round my hand.

Samantha Neish

ANOTHER TIME . . . ANOTHER PLACE

Once my name was Little Red Deer,
Won't you set my people free
We were children of the wild wind
We must be what we must be.

Once we roamed the plains together
Then the white man came along
And he built his chains and fences
Tried to tell us we were wrong.

But we knew the signs in nature
We loved the river and the sky
And our fathers long before us
Said we must beside them lie.

Then my name was Amy Cohen
Won't you set my people free
We a nation without country
We must be what we must be.

When the darkest days descended
And the world ignored our cries
As we huddled close together
Underneath those reddened skies.

Now a people with a purpose
In the land of Galilee
Where the olive branch now flourish
We will be what we will be.

Now my name is Bridie Murphy
Won't you set my people free
In my country still divided
We must be what we must be.

Once we starved along the ditches
Driven from our land and home
Many sailed across the water
Like a child torn from the womb.

Will we ever be united?
Where all four parts will be one
Will our people live together?
Underneath a common sun.

Gerard Martin

THE OLD DAYS

We met, we married a long time ago
We worked long hours for wages so low.
No telly, no wireless no bath, things were hard
No hot water - a cold tap up the yard.
No holidays abroad, no carpets on floors,
We had coal on the fire, never locked doors.
Our children arrived no pills those days.
We brought them up without state-aid.
They were safe to play in the park
And old folk could walk in the dark,
There were no drugs, Valium, LSD.
We curbed our ills with a cup of tea.
If you were sick, you were treated at once
Not fill in forms, come back in six months.
No vandals, muggings, there's nothing to rob,
But we were happy with a couple of bob.
People were happier in those far off days
Kinder and caring in so many ways.
Milkmen and paper-boys used to sing
A night at the pictures was a mad fling.
We had our share of trouble and strife
We had to face that position in life.
Now I look back over the years
I remember the blessings and the tears.

Sheila Waller

HOW TIME EVOLVES

Music's free to fill our heart,
Decades pass through the arts,
Tinkling sun passes the silent moon,
At sometime between just past noon.

Spring colours of dust and earth,
Breed new signs of life and birth,
The air smells of quickening pace,
When lines and wrinkles show on your face.

The heat comes beating hard,
Life in the balance of the remaining card,
Hard stares and eyelid glances,
When rushing souls pass by new advances.

Browns and yellows fly lifelessly past,
Clock's hands scrap while turning fast,
Warm and soft is their breath on the air,
Cosily tucked up in their bedding of care.

Wintry death can be just a heartbeat away,
Flickering light into our day,
A brandy bottle a whisky glass,
Entering souls pure as brass.

A passionless night and a wintry shrug,
And silently a hand pulls the plug,
A swirling mass of ice lies lame,
Stays cool in peace, but melts near flame.

Sharon Brick (15)

MEMORIES

Summers past in long ago days
When time stood still.
Vibrant hours that lasted forever.
Childhood's embrace, clinging fast
To the straining hands of the clock.
Halting their eternal journey
At least for a while.

A vast, shimmering expanse of speckled stones.
Crunching soothingly underfoot.
Teaming lakes of sparkling gravel.
Catching beams of light as they playfully dance
Thrown out carelessly, by a younger summer sun.
Cascading images of light and sound that make up.
The grand entrance to the paradise that once lay beyond.

Paradise lost, but not forgotten.
Imprinted on the celluloid of childhood memory.
Flashing through consciousness in vivid colour.
A familiar friend returns, the warm glow
Ignited without fail, by the sound
Of footsteps, on gravel.
Pictures spring to life, the reel of film begins
Comfort evoked by the crunching

Of stones underfoot
The heavenly harmony of which
Is the key that unlocks the cerebral gateway
To the secret garden beyond.
Paradise remains, for my eyes only.
No-one else can enter the lost garden
Suspended in time, caught and held forever.
Like a butterfly in a schoolboy's jar.

Joanna Malone

DAD'S PRECIOUS BIKE

Mum wondered why Dad was late that day
But did not worry, he'd be on his way
It wasn't like Dad to be this late
Then we heard the sound of an engine at our gate

Mum went to the window and got a surprise
Neither mum or I could believe our eyes
Standing at the gate all shiny and black
Was the Co-op hearse with Dad's bike in the back

Well as you can imagine my mum nearly fainted
As she stared at the hearse that had newly been painted
There was Dad and Bob in the front seat
The bike in the back all nice and neat

A very reserved person my mum's always been
Embarrassed she looked or so it would seem
She raced downstairs to wait for Dad
Poor soul he was about to be told off real bad

As Dad and Bob parted I've never seen the like
When in the gate came Dad and his precious bike
Mum started as soon as the door was shut
Poor Dad just kept saying but, but, but

When mum finished her long moan
Dad shook his head and let out a groan
Said he 'A puncture had burst my front tyre
When along came Bob in his private hire'

As usual he managed to bring mum around
No truer love in this world could be found
Although they disagreed over many things
They were proof of what true love really brings

Often I remember this story and smile
The day Dad took a lift to save walking a mile
I'm sure he saw the funny side knowing what he was like
And I will never forget the Co-op hearse and Dad's precious bike

Janette McCabe

EARTHLINGS 3001

Scientific laboratories on the moon,
Travelling time,
Midnight to noon,
Contact made with alien beings,
Sexless, six fingered creatures,
All slimy and green,
Solar cars are quiet and clean,
No pollution to be seen,
Rainforests are a major attraction
To see something natural,
Is pure satisfaction,
Population decreased by one child only,
Boy or a girl,
Your choice of two,
Born with perfection,
And measured IQ,
Religion is just a thing of the past,
Nothing defies the logic of maths,
Remote controlled limbs,
Replace what we've lost,
War and destruction,
We're counting the cost,
We search for a planet,
The same as our own,
So we can live,
In a nature free zone!

Sandra G Blackburn

OUR DELCIE

There once was a lass name of *Delcie,*
Who no papers would ever get rid.
To get out of the rubble
that caused all the trouble
She would run off quite reg'lar to *Brid.*

Her weekly art class it was special,
With paint brush and pencil she'd strike.
And with care and finesse,
And her can of Guinness,
She'd have made Van Gogh get on his bike.

Calligraphically she'd go her way,
To spread out her talents still wider,
But too many such clubs,
And likewise the pubs,
Leave words like a demented spider.

The Arthritics were where it began,
Where she'd knit and she'd brew and she'd sew.
it were all a big con,
'Cos she'd got nothing wrong,
since they cut off her grotty big toe.

But her passion in life's not yet stated,
Where she always sets her sights high;
Our Delcie's Jet-set,
(though they never get wet),
Can be found in the RNLI.

Boris

BISEXUAL AGE

The future is here,
It's stareing along a four year track.
Our sense of apprehension,
leads us to falter and
look back.
Not in contempt or tragedy,
but with loss of childhood
wandering.

The naive are flogged for
their purity.
And bodies are becoming one,
Like a Holy Trinity.
Trinity of minds,
curved with intricate virtual realities,
and bygone windows,
but who will we show.
Come in and sit
and view the new bisexual age.
Where sex, music and sellotape
mingle.
Like a collage of faces etched into a wall.
Gaping mouths and last
breathed farewells.
The end of this time is
the start of the new time.
So reach out and
Step inside.

Keely Mills

CONSIDER GRANDMAMA

What a mess this country's in today,
Caused by the greed of man I'd say.

We've never had so much before,
Why do we all keep wanting more?

Poor granny never travelled far,
But then she never had a car,

Now there's one at every door,
And fitted carpets on our floor.

While granny had her cocoa mats,
Cloth pegged rugs or wooden slates,

And I am sure she'd swap with glee,
Her crystal set for our TV.

On wash day she for hours would rub,
The clothes against broad in washing tub.

No machine to wash rinse and spin,
No dryers warm to put clothes in.

A hot brick paper wrapped instead,
Of electric blanket warmed her bed.

She cooked upon a coal range black
No auto-time or thermostat.

No holiday abroad had she
But just a day spent by the sea.

No pill or loop condom or coil,
But self control for one and all.

The list is endless you must see
That you are better of than she.

So please would all you moaners stop
And really look at what you've got?

Jean Roughton

PAST WAYS

Clover and coarse grass
Cows grazing as in centuries past
I wonder how long this will last

Quiet summer days with warm haze
The fields of corn in their glory blaze
The horse and plough all gone now
Tractors we drive with their awful row

Ploughing a field in a day
Never allowing in the children to play
Progress this is so they say
I preferred the slow pleasant way

Smelling of earth and fresh mown hay
Washing the sweat from your body away
A well earned rest at the end of the day
Going to bed tired but happy you sway

Today once again is brand new
Put on the kettle make a brew
Out in the fields still lots to do
But much satisfaction when finished feel you

Anne Brodie

1930-40 THROUGH A CHILD'S EYES

I grew up in Walthamstow
East of London town
Not far from the River Lea
Where sticklebacks could be found

A crowded street market
Full of hustle bustle and noise
It was all part of the fun
When they chased away us boys

I remember the old tram cars
That travelled along the rails
The coalman with his horse and cart
We boys followed with our pails

When we had earned some pennies
There was a dash to the candy shop
To buy a hapeth of sherbet dip
And a coloured whip and top

Saturday night my gran would say
Take my jug and get me some stout
If I said I didn't want to
She'd give my head a clout

Also a basin of peaspudding
You pass the shop on your way
You will get a penny for going
So don't you go taking all day

Then there was November the fifth
By the railway station they would try
To blacken up my face whilst in a pram
It was an honour to be the guy

You are told about the hardships
True in many ways
But I will lovingly remember them
As the good old days

F H G Fuller

A LAMENT FOR LOST TRANQUILLITY

The small cottage with old oak door
Has stood for a hundred years or more
By the junction of road and narrow lane
With glorious views from each window pane.
No gamekeeper stalks the rabbits now
No wind turns the sails of the mill
No lock-keeper works at the waterside
The old lock gates are still.
Noisy tractors frequent the road
Which the shire horses trod
The helicopter with deafening sound
Swoops and sprays chemicals on the ground.
The quiet road has given way
To traffic speeding to motorway.
Sweet bird-song is often drowned
By ear shattering awful sound
Of aircraft returning from abroad
Their suntanned passengers to unload.
The church clock strikes the hour of day
Below, in their graves, old villagers lay,
One wonders what they all would say
About speed and noise of present day.

Q Fowles

TIME WILL

It seems time marches on, elusive as it is it turns on
like the hands of a clock in circumference,
it winds on into infinity, the cosmos wandering on,
star to star, they glow in the darkness, the light of night,
in the eternal, the light,
are we any closer or just light years away.

Infinite, like a space, outer and inner space,
the presence of God in the universal, a scattering of stars,
so vast, far away, you and I, are we, is it at an end.

Mentor, mysterious, God without end, is eternity,
it reaches out like the hands of a clock
in the darkness.

This light that is, come into the world, for all.

Robert Robb

VALLEYFIELD PIT DISASTER

They paced up and down
Praying for hope
asking dear Lord
How will we cope?

The pit had
given way
to claim the lives
for today

Men lost their lives
to leave their
loved ones
to struggle and strive

Elizabeth Marshall

THE FARRIER'S TALE

From where does it come this divine inspiration?
The blacksmith sighs in resignation
The anvil takes its daily punishment
The hot steel cries out in repent
Bending, glowing, melting, shaping
Those hands of pure imagination
Malleable wrist on wrought iron frame
Pumping the bellows stoking the flame
Sweat pouring from that furrowed brow
That fashioned the horseshoe that spawned the plough
A craft preserved and handed down
To the next generation of this town
Where horses once clip-clopped the streets
And coal was the main source of heat
Chestnuts roasting on a blackened shovel
Cleared his mind of toil and trouble
The shire horse had its day and went
Passing of an era we can now lament.
The flash of spark the glow of ember
'Twas a sight we would long remember.

Alan K Fowles

WHY?

Why
Why is the world so bitter and sad?
Why is it senseless, deranged and mad?
Why is there killing, bloodshed and tears?
Why are there thousands living with fears?
Why is there hatred, famine and war?
Why the atrocities that no one saw?

How can man develop a taste
for things that are clearly very debased?

Vincent-Wayne Mitchell

RETURN TO THE PAST

When day is done and all is still
And the moon is on the wane
My thoughts go back into the past
To childhood's scene again.
As on the wing they rise and fly
It gives me joy to see
That all I loved so long ago
Return once more to me.

The cottage where the clematis twined
Round the white washed wall
My mother standing by the door
The dearest scene of all.
My father driving home the sheep
The dog trotting by his side
To rest when day's labour ends
In the hush of eventide.

Once more the scene was changed
I hear my brother call
I see him standing on the green
With cricket bat and ball
I see us once more upon the swing
Flying through the air
Then chasing the butterflies
Hovering round us there.

The years may come the years may go
But memories will forever last
God gave us the gift of thought
For remembrance of things past.

Mary Ferguson

HAPPY MEMORIES

Remember the days when you were young
To gladden and lighten days thro' life
When each day seemed a bundle of fun
Happy times that brought on a laugh
Every morn when off you would race
Should you miss something going on
Never time for a tear on your face
From dawn until the sunset had gone

Happy all day not thinking of rest
When the sun vanished and darkness fell
Then you scurried home to your nest
Looking so vibrant and seemingly well
Then off to bed to rest and dream
Magic dreams all through the night
Come the dawn up with a charming gleam
Starting another day of sheer delight

Rarely a dull moment in your life
No stress nor care to bring you woe
Just carefree days filled with delight
Freedom from many an uncaring foe
Those unforgettable days may be long passed
But should remain alive in your heart
To give courage in life to the last
Happy memories held dear not to depart.

Josephine Foreman

RETURNING HOME

The horse-drawn carriage pulls up,
in front of their Tudor style home,
soft snow has fallen,
white frosty foam.

Their driver tugs,
at the polished brass handle,
after a generous tip of the hat,
he quickly assembles the red mat.

Mi Lord and Lady step down,
welcomed by the snowy scene,
          Lord Edgar exclaims;
                    This is obscene!

They must be careful not to fall,
so Clive walks them to the door,
          Lady Brittany marvels,
          at what the others wore;
          Those creamy taffetas,
                    such sinful silk,
          most lovely lacy ribbons,
          the bold bustier of Lady Wilk!

It's all in a night's socialising,
the burgundy's gleam and fire's spark,
they dress in their night clothes,
and the lights turn dark.

Eva Byzio

THE FUTURE - THE END

The future portrays the book's last page,
Last chapter at its close
There's no way that we can turn back
And everybody knows
That it's our fault
We're at this stage,
God's roles for us
So badly played.

The land so stricken with disease,
It's brought the people to their knees.
The scattering of trees, so sparse,
We hardly dare to breathe
Nature's creatures all extinct
We've hunted down the lot
Slaughtered them for petty use
When we knew that we should not.
And now there's nothing left to do
Than stare at empty space
And dream of all our yesterdays
And generations waste.

Sandra Findlay

TIME

Time goes on, and still my dear - I miss you
No one to hold, and make me bold - I miss you
When life crowds in, with all its din - I need you
When I feel old, and life is cold - I need you
My dearest one, there is no sun, no love, no fun,
How long, how long, must I go on - without you?

June Eckfelt

DREAM WITH ME

Just close your eyes and dream with me,
It's 1952.
The war is over, and food still rationed,
But we've enough to see us through.
Our one ounce of cheese and eight
pennyworth of meat
Joined our weekly ration of tea.
Our empty new kitchen cabinet
Just sat there for all to see.
We got one up on the Joneses.
With our £900 Hunter Hawk,
But weren't allowed much petrol
So often still had to walk.
Under £2000 bought a new semi,
But only men could buy.
Women weren't allowed a mortgage
But heaven alone knows why.
At bathtime we had a giggle
In our four inches of water allowed;
There was a chilling gasp if you got in last,
So it didn't pay to be proud.
Mother dressed in her twin set
Managed the average weekly £9.
We were denied the pleasure of TV,
The £90 just couldn't be found.
But family life was happy,
Hyperactivity was unknown.
We made our own entertainment,
Content to stay at home.
Come on - wake up! - Your dream is over.
It's 1992.
This is a materialistic world,
But has it bettered you?

Val Patten

CHILDHOOD MEMORIES

Toasted crumpets on an open fire
Stew and dumplings, bacon and onion pud,
Cocoa made in a chipped enamel jug
and served in my favourite mug.
The smell of home-made cakes and bread
and all the fairy stories that I'd read.
Fresh vegetables picked from the garden
and picking up eggs from our dear old hen.
Collecting the milk straight from the cow,
icicles hanging from the window ledge
and the milkman's horse who ate our hedge.
Queuing for some oranges and a tin of fruit
mum making my brother a grey flannel suit.
Rainwater from the butt for washing our hair
and a lump of carbolic which we had to share.
A Sunday best dress for Sunday school
and a pink silk hankie from Uncle Bill,
wooden toys at Christmas made by dad
a stocking hanging from our beds,
on Christmas morning we would take a look
to find sweets and nuts and a lovely book.
Frosty mornings sometimes snow
my new baby sister coming home
wrapped in a blue fringed shawl.
Just some of the things I remember
when I was small.

Sheila Page

VISITING THE GRANDPARENTS

It was love at first sight to my infant eyes
White sails of the mill against the skies
The smithy, the coppice, the village green
And the home that once my father's had been.

A well in the garden, a pump and a tap,
A privy and coalhouse combined,
A profusion of flowers all colours and kinds
And trellis where roses climbed.

To my mind bright pictures I still recall
Of a Christmas that was to one so small
A magical time though not understood,
But something that was so wonderfully good.

A room warm and snug I remember
A bright kitchen range and a fender,
A feast on the table and we all found our place
As grandfather solemnly said 'The Grace'.

Happy days as I grew older
Summer visits we made each year,
I cycled the lanes with my father
Loving the peace that was here.

Very flat and black the Fenlands
And the wind so constantly near
Moaning over the farmlands
A sad voice that for ever I'll hear.

In old age I reflect and reminsce
So quickly gone those years of bliss,
Yet still I remember love's first kiss
And all our simple happiness.

Now autumn has gone and winter is here
It's a time to remember those who were dear
The faces we loved and the places too
A time to give thanks for the joys that we knew.

Margaret Copeman

WHEN I WAS A CHILD

When I was a child there was lots to do,
There was no time for sniffing glue.
We'd ride our bikes along the lane,
And down the street, some would complain.
Hopscotch, skipping, playing ball,
Especially rounders fun for all.
Occasionally we would be bad,
Say a swear word, heard from dad.
When it was late we'd hurry home,
For mum had told us not to roam.
On the table bread and jam,
A cup of tea, some chips and Spam.
No talk of drugs like LSD,
Pot was a thing in which to pee.
No talk of rape, or having it away,
Kiss chase was a game we'd play.
Behind the bike shed maybe a cig,
We only did that to be big.
A shame we started smoking, still,
We never knew that it could kill.
I wish those days did still remain,
For what today have we to gain.
From the violence, we see on TV,
Those happy days no more to be.

Pamela Stone

COMPUTER GENERATION

Click, and you'll find me down the line
In byte size pieces of binary rhyme,
On a world-wide web of words that weave
Ideas to share and some to leave.

In with the crazies surfing the net
Riding the wave without getting wet,
An escape into space from reality
A virtual world, virtually free.

Processor, chip and fibre optic,
A mouse to hold and double click
Better love the CPU
à la mode, the modem too.

Travellers on the super highway
Switch off, disconnect and walk away
Access the world with love as a guide
Connect with life and step outside.

Christine Gosling

TOMORROW, YESTERDAY AND TODAY

May today last forever
May tomorrow never come
For yesterday's already forgotten
But today must go on and on

Now must be eternal
Soon threatens to arrive
Then lingers vague and distant
Now fights to stay alive

When time no longer matters
Then time is ebbing away
A lifetime spent in a second
Tomorrow, yesterday and today

Elaine El-Masri

TIME

Time transcends dimensions beyond,
Time travellers merging past with future in the present,
Time wasters measuring with clocks and calendars.

Nature's time by seasons changing
Lunar cycles, constellations,
The vast uncharted universe
May be functioning in reverse time
Infinite and limitless
At the core.

When it passes, where does it go?
Why stay still? Why fly sometimes?
How can it be right or wrong time
Inconvenient? Unfortunate?
Can you be born before your time?

It does not hang alone:
Connotations contort,
Constrain it
Into space
That does not exist
In reality
Lost in time.

Rhiannon Phillips

PAST PROBLEM OR FUTURE PROBLEM?

Once upon a time this land smelt green,
The air was fresh and trees could be seen.
Over the hills were blue skies and pools,
Insects reflect off pretty toadstools.
But things change a lot;
With time they rot.

Factories developed and smoked out the town,
People covered their faces to avoid coming down!
Diseases spread and there were no cures,
Cholera and typhoid proved conditions weren't pure.
Things then changed quick,
Who's to die? Take a pick!

Later on then came the big world wars,
Ruins and smoke, devastation's an eyesore!
People depressed, their communities wrecked;
Death all around everyone's upset.
Things change for the worse,
Later on, the smells disperse.

We all have cars, use buses and planes.
All this stuff kills, are we insane?
What once smelt green and fresh and pure,
Now is all dying, but there's no cure.
No way to stop it, only slow it down,
It will be gone, what was once our town!

Carla Griffiths

OUR STREET

Cobbled road, brutal to unshod feet
Running, with laughter in the air
Rosy cheeks chilled by the cold
Dancing in the streets without a care

Homes inviting, no door closed
With flagstones scrubbed until white was found
A shop dwells proudly on the corner
And grandma would often pop round

Cupboards empty, but a meal created
A delicious aroma drifted down our street
Aprons adorned a plump waist
Preparing a delicacy without any meat

Busy mothers at their windows
Watching their bairns at play
Out until the dark descends
Inciting sweet dreams until another day

No toys displayed in children's bedrooms
One wage would not go far
Never had, was never missed
No such luxury of a car

A noble policeman on every turn
To escort us safely to school
Respect was in abundance then
Lack of money maybe! But our life was full.

Jane C Cook

THIRTEEN YEARS ON

Can you see the pain
in the slits of my eyes?

Last night my neighbour
was robbed in her sleep.

This morning
the insular city
casts its eyes away
stepping over her white outline;
a chalk ghost,
a chewing gum dot-to-dot
sprawled across the boulevard's familiarity.

Can you see the pain
in my white knuckled fists?

Last night my neighbours
were burnt in their sleep;
the man next door didn't like what they said.

I watch the smoke rise
from the skeleton-black beams
and ask:
how long can this go on?

Benjamin Jones

PAST LOVE

Why have I loved you
For so many years?
Why do I still think of you,
And can still shed tears?

Memories of the past,
For a love that will always last,
Though we have to be apart
My love for you
Is always in my heart.

Patricia Bullock

WARTIME CHILD

Daddy away
Occasionally
Came home on leave
Kissed mum and me.

Curtains lined black
Concealing light
From German planes
At dead of night.

The sirens wail
Fills you with fear
Blessed relief
Come the all clear.

Trips to the shops
With ration books
Dried powdered milk
Challenging cooks.

Barrage balloons
Grey in the sky
Threatening foes
Up there on high.

Daddy returns
Eventually
A stranger now
To mum and me.

Jenni J Moores

BEFORE IT'S TOO LATE

Barren land
Stretches out before us.
There is no sign of life.
Trees, all gone.
No grass,
No birds,
No people.
Our future is nothing.
Let us change it now
Before it's too late.

Jennifer Emery

MOSAIC FLOORS AND SHINY WELLIES

pale green paint, plaster walls
coloured coats on iron pegs
anoraks, duffel bags
shiny wellies, little legs
window ledges, plastic mugs
thirsty mouths to drink
soap that had a certain smell
'carbolicky' and pink
roller towels, stripy borders
little sinks, mosaic floors
paper towels, wire mesh bins
overflowing behind the doors
dormant memories flooding back
always knew they would
mosaic floor, shiny wellies
school cloakroom, my childhood

Carole Jones

FUTORIA

The cities are made of steel,
The walls are made of glass,
Magnets have replaced the wheel;
And weather doesn't make any difference,
We all live undercover in our automatic atmosphere,
Full of self-control
Governed by those who steer.

They call this town Space, Four-Nine,
We've all got jobs, it's like doing time,
Surveillance cameras are all around,
Watching, listening for my every sound.

We get synthetic rain,
The sun is made of brass,
Doctors have replaced pain;
And individuals don't make any difference,
We are little computer people on a giant microchip,
Flying through our lives,
On a nuclear powered rocket ship.

Does everyone love living life like this?
Nothing going wrong, no more hit and miss,
There is no such thing as poverty,
Crime and violence don't even feature on my TV.

Futoria,
If it is not in the future,
Then it can't be in the past,
Perhaps it's all in your head.

B Holland

THE FUTURE

Almost everyone is thinking about their future
A future that will make them happy forever
But to get that we must come together
And as things change it gets harder and harder

We all want the best future for our children
And this is a corrupt world so we must be careful in what we show them
The future is ahead of us
And it only could get better or worse

Look what we've done to the world - look what we are doing to our children's future
Everyday we hear news about a disaster
Everybody wants to rule the world
And everybody wants to be in control

The future is not the present, the future is in time to come
And some people want all, some people might never get some
Because life on earth is not fair
And because some of us are poor our kids might not have their share

Nobody knows what the future holds for them
Because we are all different, we are not the same
But because we suffered in the past and present, we wonder about our children's future
Wondering if life will get better or harder

Some of our future is gone, it's the kids that are the leaders of tomorrow
So let us prepare happiness for them, not sorrow
No-one knows what the future world will be like in time
It's only God who knows what is next in line

In this future some kids or people could have all the joy
While some suffer and cry
In my days there was no future, there was no plan so my future lost
So that's why in this great future I can't forget my past

In the present there was so much hate and anger
If only we knew that the future will have love and good all over
And for the future to come we should teach the children love and not crime
Because life is one big road with lots of signs

Michael Sylvester

AGE IS TIMELESS

Take a good look around you now.
At the things within your life.
Twenty long years have passed you by.
Now you've a family, and a wife.

It doesn't seem that long ago.
That you were out with the lads.
Now when you pass them in the street.
They've all turned into dads.

When you were ten you joined the Cubs.
When you were twenty you were thrown out of pubs.
You made it to thirty.
So what do you care.
You cruised up to forty.
Now you're losing your hair.
They surprised you with a party.
When you reached fifty.
You never stopped moaning.
When you made sixty.
You're amazing, you still drive a car.
Now you are seventy.
Now you've reached eighty.
You've slowed right up.
It takes you an hour, just to get up.
Ninety it came, and went with a flash.
Yes! You made it to a hundred,
But, fell asleep at the bash.

Derrick Evers

NOT ANY MORE

On cold November mornings I stop and take a look
At the faded, yellow pages of my history book
It doesn't seem long since I saw the open door
I took all these chances but not any more
I turn back time and it hurt enough then
But for you I'd go through it all over again
It could have been forever
But it never
Had a chance to live

I think of what a fool I was and slowly shake my head
All those hopes and dreams, and like the summer they lie dead
They look at me - yes, they've seen me here before
I used to walk along this road, but not any more
I got it really bad but I'm going to stand my ground
I'm going to make sure that there's no one else around
It could have been forever
But it never
Had a chance to grow

I look back as I walk down Memory Lane
Just another tragedy but I can't ignore the pain
Like another piece of driftwood washed up on the shore
I used to play along with you, but not any more
Looking all around I ask myself and wonder how
I ever trusted you but that was then, this is now
Yes it could have been forever
But it never
Had a chance at all

Kate Kivlichan

BACK TO THE FUTURE

They say the past is dead and gone, and there is no need to look back,
But sometimes we cannot help but think, either good, bad, busy or slack,
Sometimes in the past, we go through thick or thin, rain, sun or shower
But happy and carefree times were there, as we flourish like a flower.

The saying was, hard work never killed anyone, that is what it was like
in the past
Laughter, jokes and good humour shared, something that money couldn't
buy at any cost
Neighbours helped one another, or just went in for a cup of tea,
Especially in my mother's day, nobody was frightened, you see,
Going back to my young school days, my mother could leave a key
through the door,
But coming back here to the present, we daren't do this any more.

There are too many crooks around, this day.
Too much crime performed at bay,
We look at the news on television, somebody has done something really bad,
Has this very day and present, and time gone mad.

But the present could be fine for all, and my friends and me.
Through God's love, so wonderful, rich and free,
if only those such people could come to terms from bad to good,
Then the world and community would be like it should,
For such people could be nice and friendly, and help one another,
Then the present could be far better.

If everyone could think there is a heaven ahead,
The present and future could be so wonderful, instead,
If we could just see and look what happened in the past again,
For the love of the most high God, we can all regain,
The future the present and back to the past,
There will be happiness and peace at last.
if we work out from the past, to the present, once more,
Then we come once again back to the future.

Jean McGovern

THE GOOD OLD DAYS

We could walk on our own
Down a country lane
Without fear of attack
That is now life's bane.

With a pound in our pocket
For our weekly bill
We could eat like kings
With no need of pills.

But, there was still unemployment
And queue's for the dole
Babies died for starvation
And no money for coal.

The rich just got richer
While the poor died like flies
Maybe life's not much different
We still hear the same cries.

Marjorie Horgan

REMEMBER WHEN

Entering into the forest of a dream
Searching not knowing what I'm searching for,
Babbling brook fabricated out of a thought,
I cup and fill my hands to take a drink,
As they are raised up the reflection isn't mine,
There staring back is the most beautiful vision ever seen.
Not a word passes her lips as she smiles
And the smile says so much
It's then I realise I've drunk from a pool of memories.

Stephen Poole

YEAR 2400

With slow rhythmical movements the students deeply dug
Twentieth century life had been geared to the thug,
Ruined buildings revealed parts of old guns, rusty now
Broken needles and syringes were all used somehow.

In history we had learnt people then took a fix
To get stoned out of their senses with a powder mix,
Gradually destroyed each country through greed and war
What a legacy left for us from those gone before.

The twenty-fifth century is bringing such new hope
In this day and age natural living makes sure we cope.
Prime cattle, crops, vegetables all flourish at last,
We use normal day-time and night-time not like the past.

Mary Beale

THE FUTURE

Pink and blue cumulus clouds
Floating in the summer sky.
What does the future hold
For you and I?
Will the wind of adversity
Blast us away?
Or will we sail on
With the summer zephyr
That bears up eagles' wings
And brings the sailing ship
Back home again?

Jenny Cox

DAYS OF FUTURE PAST

Jules Verne and HG Wells
Had visions of a future unseen,
What had seemed science fiction
Is no longer coming, it's been.

When I was but a young lad
They wanted a man on the moon
And within the space of a year
We knew it was coming, and soon.

Now we have reached the nineties
The future has become our past,
Man's now striving for the stars,
It's no longer coming, it's been.

There really is no future,
We never actually get there,
It's always only the present,
And everything else is past.

Raymond Lewis

FADING MEMORIES

Watching the sunset fade away
say farewell to another day,
A day that's full of heartache
a day that's full of pain,
Reminiscing my memories
of a love that used to reign,
But fading with the sunset
are my memories of old
my special treasured memories
that once were as precious as gold.

Sandra Nicholls

SPRING FLOWERS

When I was a girl, of ten years old
To walk in the country, we were told
My brother and I, its beauty to behold
So after Sunday school, still in Sunday best
To stroll in the park, through the woods
In the stream, such delight
Bluebells, violets beneath our feet
Such a lovely, colourful sight
Along the lane, daffodils, oh so pretty
To not take some for mother
Would be such a pity
Just a few, I'll stoop to pick
In a jar with bluebells, just the trick
A tap on the shoulder, a voice I heard
What are you up to, my pretty miss
Oh what a shock! I dropped the lot
Miss Morris, my headmistress, standing there
Those flowers are in my garden dear
Now you've picked them, keep them
But don't pick them again, it's private here
At home on the window-sill, they looked so pretty
Monday morning was my face red
When in assembly, Miss Morris said
How beautiful she thought the daffodils
Near her home, this spring
But they're not for picking, whenever I see daffodils
Growing in the wild, my thoughts return
To when I was a child.

Irene Corbett

FLOWER POWER

Free love, flowers and beads
substances taken and parents agreed
to disagree on their children's views
choosing to condemn the life they choose
condemning the reasons to draw away
from the monotonies lived each single day
but the children listened not
for escapism was the name of the game
flaunting their independence without worry or shame

Free love, free love . . flowers and beads
hair flowing loosely, hair and creeds
stating points, stating a way
to get up in the morning, look forward to the day
whilst politicians condemned they who hemmed
the followers into corners
but as like little Jack Horner
they stuck up their fingers
and said in your world we will not linger

For in your world there are rules . . .
rules of your making
and as in your schools
they leave us shuddering and quaking
and we may not have it right, only time will tell
but man we feel freer than living in your hell
so we take freedom of expression and use it thus
for we are being who we want to be . . .
and that is us . . . just us

Kathleen Schmidt

FADING

Blink and it's gone
The dark fields of my mind hold many hells
Think the moment and you lose her
Time, the traitor laughing
Searching, I catch a fragment, beauty
A child-rose
A thousand kisses into the hazy blue
A whisper, a promise, a lie
A time insular, basic, hungry
Then wondrous, open
The original sin of my mother
And my father, leaving,
Staking the way for future betrayal
Child, wet-faced, laughing
Brother, school, home
Deeply wounded by my childhood passing
A slow-time dancing allows a smile
A birth, my own flower
A marriage, my own jailer
A loss; my tears dried with my milk
A timeless grieving, sorrow
Constriction, restriction, murder, terror, hell
Into insanity, illness
I kicked the soil with my toes from the noose
Vomiting the years of his acid smile
And now this present has become the past
Recovery, discovery, sanity
The monsters no longer hold me
My dreams are healthy
And now we smile

Rachel Sprason

1996

Are our descendants meeting up with our ancestors
And seeing us in the middle
An interesting riddle
Giving us food for thought with
So many strange reports
2151 and 1751
Two hundred years back and
Two hundred years on
Forty-five years on
To date
Celebration!
Could this change the face of
The whole nation
Today!
Could it be God's creation?

Kathryn Longley

JUST A MEMORY

Yesterday is just a memory
A memory from the past.
And now the past is over
But will the memory last?
A memory can live forever
Engraved inside your mind,
But the past will never change
As it's all been left behind.

Amanda Brown

TODAY'S TEENAGERS

Don't they want to make you swear,
Telling us what they want to wear,
Their friends come in and play about,
My husband swears and I do shout,
I know that when I was that age,
My parents would get in a rage,
The kids today expect a lot,
For money which we have not got,
So off they go to find a job,
Or else they might become a yob,
In the evenings, where do they go,
To the park or some disco,
Coming home in the early hours,
We keep on saying, 'They can't be ours,'
But we did it years ago,
Go through it again, no! No! No!

Pat Garvey

THE TAKE-OVER

Streets carpeted by homeless families
Jobs once theirs,
Now a machine's.
Technology takes over
No one ever satisfied
With the present situation
Always wanting new machines
Meaning more lost jobs.

Naomi Westwood

IN DAYS GONE BY

Imagine what it would be like
To have lived in times gone by
Up at dawn and bed at dusk
All your life until you die
Farming the land using brute strength
Pulling a heavy plough
Sowing the seeds and reaping the crop
Feeding and milking the cows
Everything had to be cooked from scratch
And shopping was not very good
It was a very long walk to the village
And there was no money for food
The women had to make the clothes
And also weave the cloth
They also looked after the family's health
From the measles to a cough
Every day was a hard days work
With exercise aplenty
Lifting, fetching, carrying, and walking
Miles upward of twenty
There was no retirement then
It was a family affair
Even when great-grandad got too old
He supervised them from a chair.

Sonia Gillings

BITTER-SWEET

The scene of Earth was bitter-sweet,
The roads were gone as were the streets.
No cities, buildings, power plant left,
No vehicles, no planes, no fleets.
All that was left was tall green grass,
Strong flowing rivers, blue skies at last.

The people too were long since gone,
Just animals left and nice bird songs.
Man's dream of future left no sign,
His wars had killed it for all time.

Paul Sanders

SEARCHING

Stand with your back
to the future
Don't look behind you yet
Gather the dreams
That you spun like a web
Tomorrow is chance - don't forget

An eye searching to be recognised
Captures the past
With its dreams and behold
Atmospheres of suspense
Sadness and joy
Were there to catch
and hold.

And now turn around
Memory Lane was for real
New doors ready to open
New dreams there to steal
Look for the light
It goes on forever
So go out there and fight.

Phyllis Moon

OUR ROAD

The roads that I remember, were mainly void of cars,
No thundering, blundering juggernauts, at night we saw the stars.
On Sundays, roads were empty, save the occasional car.
The only sound was church bells, though sometimes, that would jar.
The Boys Brigade came out in force with bugle and bass drum,
And smartly set off down the road with cheery 'tum te tum'.
On Monday mornings dustcarts came a'trundling down the street.
Shire horses pulled the brewers' drays, their nosebags full of wheat.
The rag and bone man rang his bell, awakening us from slumber
And called his plaintive cry of 'Any old rages - any old lumber.'
The milkman had a horse and cart, as greengrocer and baker,
And men politely raised their hats to hearse, and undertaker.
A sooty sweep would push his cart of brushes down the road,
And coke and coal carts tipped their sacks in cellars, to unload.
At dusk, the old lamplighter came, to fill each lamp with light.
Oh! Such a friendly mellow glow, to light us through the night.
Our streets were safe, and free from crime, none feared for their abode,
Oh how I miss that happy time, in our warm and friendly road.

Hilda Jones

A GIFT FOR THE FUTURE

In twenty years' time,
you'll be fully grown,
probably have kids
all of your own;

and how will it be,
that future for you,
surrounded by Ecstasy,
kids sniffing glue,

will you live in a fortress,
will the grass still be green,
will the birds still be singing,
the streets still be mean?

or will things have changed,
will we have learned how
to give you a future,
can we try - *now?*

Shirley Diver

AN UNKNOWN TIME

The future is ahead of me
Always another day
Never shall I catch it up
It will always be that way

What does life hold in store?
That will just take time
One day maybe I'll look back
And the past will then be mine

My destiny I can't yet see
It's an illusion of which I dream
Stretching beyond my reach
It's time that has no theme

At some point in my life
The future will be dawning
More of my life will be the past
And I'll no doubt be yawning

But here and now holds no time
The past is left behind
The things that are still yet to come
Are paths I've yet to find

Paula Stedman

MAKING MEMORIES

There's a lovely place I know
beside an old mill stream,
where memories of long ago
come back just like a dream.
It's the old allotment
where kindred spirits meet,
as many did, years before
cars blocked every street.
As I wander around this magic plot,
a rough hand takes hold of mine,
my beloved Dad is here again
spanning the bridge of time.
Once again, I'm on the bike,
cluttered with things we'd need,
my Dad in front and me behind,
in the pannier, what a steed.
We'd arrive at the shed, what excitement,
could hardly wait to get inside.
Dad went first to frighten the spiders,
they'd rush into the corners to hide.
We'd make tea on the old primus,
eat chunky bread, with strawberry jam,
sitting on the bench in the sunshine
our vegetable rows we would plan.
Dad gave me these wonderful memories
at the time I didn't see,
how much Dad gave of himself
to make memories just for me.

Audrey Packman

SHAVING SOAP

When I was a little boy
I wanted all your love.
I remember the smell of shaving soap,
when you lifted me, and put me into bed.
I still smell shaving soap,
when I go to the bathroom to pee.
Not my shaving soap,
that's from an aerosol can, bright red.
That Erasmic smell, now lost in time,
that was the smell of you,
carried over all those years, into my prime.
I felt safe when you held me dad,
high up between your arms,
and we laughed, you looking up,
me looking down, innocent and glad.

I walked behind her coffin,
but no grief or sorrow came.
I was not there for your going.
But I walked behind her in the rain.
Snowdrops were there upon your grave
nodding their Easter farewell;
I walked past you at her graveside,
and that clean, sweet, masculine, smell;
where yellow flowers lay beside her grave,
her favourites for that day.
I did not know you deeply then,
for I was only two, now after many years
I want the love I never really knew,
that evokes the essence of you.

Tom Gull

PEACE

What future, people say
It's hard enough, living today.
Just imagine what the future could hold
Strange inventions of long ago
When a rocket-ship was aimed at the moon
People scoffed, laughed and jeered
The first man on the moon must have shed some tears.
Today we could soon be reaching Mars,
Venus, Jupiter, distant stars.
Is it our destiny to probe the universe
When earth needs so much help?
Perhaps one day the world, the universe, will be united, as one
And everybody will be singing the same song:

Peace!

Annette Williams

THE EYES OF DEATH

I looked into the eyes of Death,
And liked not what I saw,
I saw only the wish for peace,
And the desire for nothing more.

The wretchedness of soul and body,
The helplessness and fear,
In speechless mouth and distant eye,
Caused me to shed a tear.

I observed Death's cloak enshroud,
And asked: 'Dear Lord, how long
Will Time wait until He takes her,
To the Land of Joy and Song?'

I feared that Time might linger,
Or, His footsteps swiftly tread.
Only a past that has no future,
Can read the eyes of Death.

Melissa Gorton

STRAWBERRY FIELDS FOREVER

The sixties was a time to swing
  A time to be sixteen
Began when Elvis was the king
  And ruled the music scene
He rock 'n rolled and sang the blues
  About His Latest Flame
A pop idol - in Blue Suede Shoes
  The Pelvis was his name

The sixties was a time to play
  Guitars - and form a band
The Beatles - had arrived and they -
  Had genius to hand
To Mathew Street they went along
  Their harmonies to share
And Liverpool burst out in song
  And music filled the air

To be part of this Happening -
  A transport of delight
To dance - Eight Days a Week - and sing
  Upon a Hard Day's Night
Those Strawberry Fields Forever stay -
  A fragrance to remind
Of dreams - in themes - of Yesterday
  And Always on My Mind

Arlene Skerratt

WILL NO ONE BOTHER CARING?

A thought about our future,
Springs images to mind.
We treat the world so wrongly,
A threat unto mankind.
With progress on the increase
Respect of earth cascades.
The survival of our planet
Meanders on to fade.
But it won't be us who suffer
We won't see the consequence
Just persistent with destruction
Have the human race no sense?
It all boils down to money.
Still the greedy do not care,
If the children of our future,
Breathe in constant poison air.
It's now we should be standing
In our mass, preserve our sphere
So the children of our future
Won't be born to live in fear.
But it's sad to face the true face
That the people in command
To save the world, are ignorant
They won't lend a helping hand.
We sit back, so long frustrated
As our earth falls now apart
Will no-one bother caring?
Such a sadness in my heart!

Charlotte Ireson

IT MUSTN'T HAPPEN AGAIN!

Boys laughing! Girls singing!
Some chatting; some swinging!
School fading - life calling!
A future enthralling!

But rumours are growing,
That war clouds are blowing.
That life, love and laughter
May vanish, hereafter.

Boys waving, girls crying,
(To smile, they are trying)
So poignant, this parting,
With dear ones departing!

Weeks passing, bombs falling!
Carnage appalling!
On shelter - folk loading,
A land mine exploding.

A message horrific!
A blow so terrific,
To young wives and mothers,
Sons, husbands and brothers.

No more'll be returning
To folk who are yearning -
A lost generation,
Whilst saving their nation!

So, for wisdom be praying!
War's slaughter, be staying!
Let peaceful relations
Return to all nations.

Nora D Jones

2050 AD (ANDROID DOMAIN)

On past events I used to reflect,
And wondered where they've gone.
Of days I walked down country lanes,
And basked out in the sun.
But since the war all that's been lost,
And mankind is no more.
Amid the blood, the sweat and tears,
A metallic race was born.

My wife and I, are the last of man.
We've lived, laughed and cried.
We've watched and fought the holocaust,
Despaired as nature died.
Android replicants now rule earth,
They caused the downfall of man.
The servers now the ones being served.
Residing, in their tin cans.

Robotic laws, where nothing grows,
Self perpetuating, mechanical rule.
Android domain, the name of the game.
Created by metallic, tyrannical fools.
Whilst humans, have lost their worth,
So against them, we must fend.
To try and recreate, man's rebirth,
Against the new age - metal men.

W Tony Crowther

LOOKING BACK

When I was a child, the winters were mild
The summers were hot, and we played a lot
And everyone smiled - when I was a child.

When I was young, love songs were sung
We danced through the night, and the world seemed all right
Church bells were rung - when I was young.

When I got married, a gas-mask I carried
The world had gone mad, and I missed my dad
To the shelters we hurried - when I got married.

When the children came life became a game
There was laughter and fun, full of days in the sun
Things were never the same - once the children came.

Now I am old, the world seems cold
But the memories last - all the joys of the past
Are there to hold - now that I am old.

E Crowhurst

EMBRYO

The future is an unborn child -
Obscure and without form.
Cradled within the darkness
Of the womb of today.
If the child will bring happiness;
If he'll bring tears or smiles,
Sunshine or raging storms,
None of us can say.

Jonathan Anstead

THE GOOD OLD DAYS

The good old days or so they say,
When just being happy was meant to be gay,
So many peculiar changes we've seen,
Not all for the best, but a changing scene.

Children don't seem to be young any more,
They're quite grown up before they are four,
They get 'tellys', computers, so very soon,
For skipping ropes, whip and tops, cut-out dolls, there's no room.

Monday was wash day, lunch - cold meat and chips,
We'd never heard of 'Dairylea dips',
On Tuesday the bedrooms were made spick and span,
The silver was polished and we'd shine every pan.

Wash day was hard with posher and tub,
And with skiffle board, we would scrub and scrub,
Then through the mangle the clothes had to go,
A back-breaking job and frightfully slow.

'Daltons' cornflakes are now no more,
You got down on your knees to scrub the floor,
There were silver sixpences, wee threepenny bits,
And the ITMA show just had you in fits.

On Sunday morn' you went for a walk,
All dressed in your best, black patents an' all,
If you were lucky, midday roast was beef,
We'd never heard of 'mad cow' disease.

Going back in time a little bit more
Out came the tin bath, it was placed on the floor
In front of the fire with coals burning bright,
What a cosy warm evening, in dim firelight.

A liberty bodice, an abbe wool vest,
Hair in 'rags' made it hard to rest.
Yet all these things we took as the 'norm',
The good old days were right on form.

Doreen Banks

DREAM OF ENGLAND

There was in England once before the fall
Of axe on tree and engine to the mine
The space to lose yourself and hear the call
Along the misty borders by a wood
To regions of past harmony divine.
Old men can still remember how they stood
Clothed in the solitude of folding light
And heard elusive music from the fields
Played by a hidden people into night.
Old farmers unobsessed by yearly yields
Have talked with trees and watched the leaves in flight
And walked the hills till morning rose again
To hide the owl and pack the stars to bed.
And there were ways to think, to walk the lane
Of linnets in the rain and swing for days
Through gate-wide hawthorn-madnesses and spring
The stiles to anywhere the morning led.
Again at hedgehog time shy birds would sing
And hide their browns in universal greys,
Then herds of royal deer beneath a moon
Would pick their way down to a bushy stream
And sniff the man, and go at once their ways.
There were such ways of going off so soon,
Old men can still remember, and I dream
Of England as she was before the fall.

Alasdair Aston

THE SHAPE OF THINGS TO COME

I'm a little tomato
All round and red
I've a cute green stalk
That sits on my head
I mostly need eating
Within a couple of days
But since scientists interfered
I've now changed my ways . . .
My shape's slowly changing
To that of a square
I suppose that it's preferable
To that of a pear
Removed is an enzyme
So now I won't rot
Hence a longer shelf life
Is what I've now got!
My friends, the bananas,
Are being turned straight
No more may they curve
Oh to be in this state!
I mean, where will we be
In some twenty odd years?
For getting carried away
Is amongst everyone's fears!
So to all you ambitious scientists out there
Remember this - nature's best left alone!
If we were meant to be straight or otherwise shaped
That's how we'd have been originally grown!

Rachael Hughes

THE OLD BRANCH LINE

The old branch line - that faithful track
Suburbia to town and back.

The old branch line - that twists and turns
Through valleys run and over burns.

The old branch line - they're closing down
I'll have to catch the bus to town.

The old branch line - that road of steel
For you my friend the church bells peel.

The old branch line - now red with rust
The memory lies in the dust.

The old branch line - long overgrown
The seed of change for you is sown.

The old branch line - the winding track
To mother nature handed back.

The old branch line - nature reserve
For butterflies and for the birds.

The old branch line - symbolic stands
In my mind's eye across the land.

The old branch line - a monument
To bygone days that came and went.

Notice:- The old branch line has been discontinued -
Due to social vandalism better known as progress.

K D Thomas

THE IDEA

Prelude
Answers, O Yeats,
Answer, dear Shakespeare.
Or better I ask
Some simple peasant
Or some arrogant majesty.

Poem
Divine Apollo, am I not thee?
Without doubt
Kavanagh would quench such a thought,
But dare I deny?

Had I the idea to travel
Back and ask the deceased
What every life would wish to know
What would I ask?
'How was life?'
'Tell me about it.'
'What truth died with you
Or created the disease
That killed you,
Or the fate that took you?'
'Where did it take you?'
'Can you answer?'

Paul Byrne

FRIENDLY GHOSTS

When it is quiet down this street
At night, and all is still,
I hear the sound of ghostly feet
I lean upon my window sill
To try and catch a glimpse
Of those
Who used to live between these rows.

A hundred years have passed by since
Each brick was placed on brick.
Mellowed with age and dark with grime
They stand in quite another time
Homely still, as when they knew
The sound of long skirts rustling through.

I wonder who first lived in here
And leant upon the window sill?
I wonder if they realised
It would be standing, useful still
When they were gone?
And who would hear the sound of them
As ghostly feet with slippers on?

Liz Pecksen

A DAY IN TIME

With stealth,
Dawns early light stains the sky,
An expectant throng grows silent,
The die is cast,
Historic events unfold,
Directives this day will be exercised,
Hooded axeman with jurisdiction carries out the excise,
Honed blade drips a gory debris,
Globules of blood so royal dawdle arcing high.

They knew not right from wrong,
A dour puritanical grasp tightens a gauntlet hold over England's realm,
In a wicker basket royal eyes fade,
The deed is done,
Charles a king is dead,
Cromwell the people's choice decreed it so,
That axeman was I so far back in time,
Regressive hypnotherapy tells it so.

Shea

TIMES PAST

I derive much pleasure browsing photographs that show
What it was like to live and work so many years ago,
The pictures of streets and places, in my city I know well,
Have changed so much in eighty years - what stories they could tell.

Some roads, almost deserted, appear so very wide
With lots of metal railings stretched all along each side,
The cars are few and far between, with occasional delivery van,
More likely it's a horse and cart, or a barrow pushed by man.

The shops draw my attention with adverts big and bold
Their windows crowded out with goods and people looking old,
The butcher stands there proudly by sides of beef and pork,
No mention of inspectors or health authority talk.

I also see the sheep which are causing quite a jam
As they take their time to wander past a patiently waiting tram,
The cattle too will pass along, toiling from the station,
Incessant probing as they walk - an hour or so's duration.

Here's a stately mansion set in grounds beside a lake,
Built in red brick and Tudor style, many servants it would take
To keep it up and running each day throughout the year,
With lots and lots of elbow grease and not a little fear!

There are courtyards, now demolished, where toddlers played of old,
With people sharing taps and toilets outside in the cold,
And lines of clothes strung up on high in order to get dry,
How many times they'd pray for sun and look into the sky.

I see beside the main road an ivy-clad building tall,
A private school for polite young ladies stands behind the wall,
Yet down in the park not far away kids paddle in the river,
A pool for boys, and one for girls - we must not mix them ever!

The photos show how rich and poor all lived their lives each day
And so it will continue as decades pass away.

Ann Collins

DO YOU REMEMBER?

Horse drawn carts for bread, milk and rubbish.
Boaters and bowlers worn with flourish.
Silver fox furs and thick tweedy skirts.
The Bisto Kids a famous advert.

Diseases were rife, killing many.
Yet, sweets and ices bought for pennies.
Chaplin and Temple, stars of the screen.
Poverty, beggars, a dismal scene.

In fields, hay stood to dry in stooks,
Walkers midst wild flowers paused to look.
We swam in rivers, rode bikes too.
Youth clubs. Outings with Sunday school.

Barges with freight of coal or timber.
Steam trains, steam ships. Ports for fish trawlers
Beach holidays with bucket and spade,
A Punch and Judy and lemonade.

Pre-war days of style and grace,
Life went at a slower pace.
War years brought doodlebugs blitz and bombs.
Munitions work, blackout, uniforms.
Rationing, just enough to eat,
Few were seen to be overweight.
Coupons for clothes and chocolate bars.
Those empty roads, when few folk owned cars.

In post-war days a National Health.
The swinging sixties and much more wealth.
Trips by air then computers and things.
Now who can tell what the future brings.

Wendy Edwards

SOAPS FROM THE PAST

Whatever happened to the soaps from years ago
Crossroads it was a regular nightly show.
It was full of problems it was full of scandal
Some of the story lines were too hot to handle.

When Jill found out that Meg had lied
That she had gone on holiday and she hadn't died.
Jill found her mum and she got a new friend,
Then that show it came to an end.

Do you remember Albion Market the Sunday soap
It got so boring I just couldn't cope.
People were wheeling and dealing all of the time
There was too much romance there was too much crime.

The Practice it came and went real quick
It was a British soap about the sick,
I enjoyed this one I thought it was good
But it got axed it was another dud.

Then there was Eldorado a British soap from Spain
They had two bit actors that just wanted fame.
The ones who were good were far too old,
Everyone I knew said that the show would fold.

And some Aussie soaps they don't last too long,
I don't think it's many but I could be wrong.
There was Richmond Hill that came and went,
It ran out of money it too quickly got spent.

I watched this soap every time it was on,
I remember it well but now it is gone.
I remember lots of soaps from back in the past,
Then they make new ones so the old ones don't last.

Angie Armstrong

CHILDHOOD MEMORIES OF TV

My TV memories start I fear
With the loud and funny fox
Called Basil Brush, boom boom
Another little friend I have
Is Orville the Duck 'I wish I could fly
Right up the sky but I can't'
Keith Harris always saying 'Yes you can'
That awful monkey Cuddles was his name
Always gave poor Orville a hard time
I remember I was always very sad
That Orville couldn't have his wish to fly
My favourite time of day was when
The Muppets came to visit
Miss Piggy swung a few punches for equality
Playschool was next on the square box
Big Ted and all his little friends
The presenters always told lots of stories
Which never failed to amuse and enchant me
When I grew up and got older
I fell in love with the world of the Waltons
Praying that my family could be like them
Longing to be part of it, to play in the fresh air
I wanted to marry John Boy, he broke my heart
And fell in love and moved away
Out of the countryside to the city
To follow his career and his love of writing
The worst memory I have of TV land
Has to be Larry 'shut that door' Grayson
Not to mention Bruce Forsyth Play Your Cards Right
And here alas my memories must come to an end

E Chambers

MY CHERUB OF DARKNESS

Death becomes her, this vision of beauty
though her heart has long ceased to beat
still her eyes hold your gaze as if magic
a place where both life and death meet

So hypnotic those orbs that you're spellbound
something dark and mesmeric, yet pure
reflecting an innocence long since passed by
(innocence makes a wonderful lure)

eternal, this vision of beauty
forever free from the shackles of time
while all who admire her, grow old, turn to dust
she remains nothing less than sublime

But this cherub of darkness has sorrow
the reason for which you can surely surmise
she must travel alone through eternity
without ever glimpsing the fire of sunrise

Tyler Bon Scott

THE DEATH STAKES

It's not a race you want to win
You'd rather continue living
Way ahead you can see a ghost
He's perched on top of the winning post

The past is behind you, so on with the race
Somebody somewhere is setting the pace
The silent procession turns into the straight
It won't be long, before you meet your fate

Your body is feeling like you've never known
When you reach the post, you'll be on your own
The saddle is heavy, but you muster a grin
You don't need the judge to tell you've weighed in

Donald Hussey

PUPPET RULERS

In days of old, when knights were bold, there was only Punch and Judy,
Oh no there wasn't, oh yes there was, everyone shouted rudely.
Then in the early fifties when I was near eleven,
I walked into our lounge at home - there stood a television.

My diction, which was never good, succumbed to 'blob a dob'
The language of Bill and Ben, and wasn't Weed quite odd?
Then there was Muffin the Mule, who on the piano danced,
And Andy Pandy who went out to play, and in the garden pranced.

Larry the Lamb spoke to Mr Mayor in a sheepish kind of way,
And Rupert and Mr Badger just passed the time of day.
Archie Andrews and Daisy May were always a good turn,
The only time that they were ill was when they had woodworm.

Basil Brush, my favourite, his catchphrase was 'boom boom'
Sooty and Sweep always seemed to have Harry Corbett in the room.
By now I was almost twenty, and at five pm not out
My friends were Florence and Zebedee, who sprang from a roundabout.

How I survived those puppets, ventriloquists and animation,
I'll never know, but at the time they absorbed an entire nation.
Now in the nineties when nights are cold, I sit thinking by the fire
Then off to the video shop I go and get Noddy out on hire!

Terence Raymond

THIS HIGHER SOURCE

Now my earthly life has run its course
My spirit to take me to this higher source.
To me there is no death,
Just a fading of a cloud.
To rest a moment in this white shroud now
As my freed spirit roars to this higher source.

I am now ready and prepared to come before
our great Creator
For He is our judge and our maker.
Now my spirit progress will surely mark my path
With the truth, love and joy I have shared,
Please, dear Lord, pave it with Thy special love and care.

I have acknowledged, and I have taught
That love is the true spirit law.
Trust in spirit - they will never let you down,
When all else fails
Our spirit angels will always
come around -

Oh! How kind the spirit whisper is,
Even though we hear no sound;
But when in dire need
Yes, we are sought and found
By this vibration of love and light.

For there is no time, in this higher source
No loud clocks, no tick-tock! Tick-tock!
But many mansions does God unlock
For those His chosen flock.

Joyce Brown

THE GOOD OLD DAYS

I recall the good old days
When I was young and free,
When money didn't matter much
And I was full of glee.
I'd sleep in, in the morning
And stay out late at night,
Have holidays in the summer
See the funfair every night.
I'd play cribbage every Monday
And darts most other nights,
Take day trips down to London
So I could see the sights.
Sometimes I would go swimming,
Watch football or play squash
It didn't matter what it cost
I'd always have the dosh.

Paul Marsden

THE AFTER WORLD

My flights of fancy are but real
In my dreams I live and have my being
Old friends and new friends I greet
Scenes so beautiful I can't believe I'm seeing
Is this my real home?
With freedom to express my love and heart's desire
Home of my thoughts, made alive and active
I greet my mum and dad, and the brother I didn't
know I had
So free am I to learn and play
When dreams become reality
This is where I would like to stay

Amy Phillips

BEYOND DREAMS

Don't sigh and don't weep,
Fond memories you keep.

Just listen carefully, don't make a sound,
I'll leave you a message, you'll
know I'm around.

I hugged you last night when you were asleep,
Tears on your pillow, please
dearest don't weep.

'The rose in the garden, that's early,'
you said,
Is this another sign or just in my head.

I like your new dress, I hasten to add,
Go out enjoy yourself, please don't
be sad.

Look on the bright side, I'm free
from all pain,
My soul still lives on, my life
'twas not in vain.

When your time comes, just reach
out your hand,
I'll be waiting to meet you, in a
far better land.

Gaenor Owens

LOST

Just blackened barren ground
and frosting air
as mud, an avalanche
rat-tails your hair -

You're standing with my letter
in your hand
remembering the day
we heard the band
exhorting fresh-faced youths like you
in August rain
to leave their loving homes
and board the train -
your country needed you
and I did, too

You didn't want to go
but knew you must -
no thought of ash to ash
or dust to dust . . .

I hear a smothered roar
smell acrid smoke
'Don't leave me now',
I almost choke

Was I wife or a widow next?
How could I tell?
Your voice
Your face (no army haircut now)
Your torch, your touch, your kiss
all broke the spell.

Joan Bulmer

SHE IS GONE!

My mummy is gone
She died today
The angels came
And took her away.
I know it was right
She was in so much pain
But my little world
Just isn't the same.
I'm shattered, I'm lost
I feel so hurt
The tears keep rolling
I've soaked my skirt.
She's up there in heaven
Looking down on me
I know she'll watch over
Together we will be.
I just wish I could hold her
And tell her I love her
Oh! I do so miss her
My dear loving mother.
She's gone, she's gone
She is now at rest
And I know deep down
It was for the best.

Mary McSweeney

REMEMBRANCE

M is for mother you were always there,
O is for only, only you really did care,
T is for toiling always baking and boiling,
H is for helping and holding and hugging,
E is for ever and ever and ever,
R remembrance, though now gone, in my mind still together.

Kevin Fitzgerald

NOT FOR THE SQUEAMISH

Hot and steamy, sticky and red,
bleeding and pulsing until you are dead.

A blood-line is broken by one single shot,
just one of the many, his blood spilled - for what?

A cold-blooded murder, her young husband dies,
a widow is grieving with blood-curdling cries.

With hot-blooded passion men rush into war
and spent bullet cases litter the floor.

It's part of the blood-bath that mankind allows,
tell that to her as his blood stains her blouse.

It's part of a blood feud, revenge satisfied,
men in their prime, how many have died?

Blood's thicker than water, children are told,
but an eye for an eye until life-blood runs cold

In the guise of justice and fairness and right,
settles nothing - but still they continue to fight,

And the victims of bloodshed through blood-shot eye,
see blood on their hands, and in torment they cry.

Pam Sowman

WHERE

Where world merges into world,
Where love replaces pain,
Where mists of emotion pass you by,
Where sun replaces rain,
Where truth shrugs off every lie,
Where lovers' hearts together stay,
Where wars have never begun,
Where they listen as we pray,
Where guiding hands reach out,
Where thoughts to us passed on,
Where dreams become so real,
Where grans and granddads have gone,
Where the children who go so young,
Where there's fields of laughter where they run,
Where there's thoughts you sent so lovingly,
Where the tears now are done,
Where everyone you see today,
Where everyone you know,
Where every living soul,
Where we all eventually go.

Kevin Cornwell

READING ABOUT YOUR ENEMIES

Reading books can change your life,
They're like gold and precious silver.
You can find out so much more
by going to a local book store.
What we read about our enemies
can change our brain and gain us knowledge.
Then our minds can store
facts we never knew before.

Ray Russell

NEVER FAR AWAY

Have you ever sat up crying
through losing someone dear?
And felt your heart would surely break
If only they were here.

The times we think about them
the love that we once shared,
of the good times and bad ones
we know how much we cared.

So let me tell you something
when all the crying's done,
as long as we have memories
they're never ever gone.

Our loved ones never leave us
they're never far away
we see them in a sunbeam
on a special sunny day.

We hear them gently whisper
from a crystal bubbling stream
and hold them even tighter
in an extra special dream.

Can we really smell them
whilst the grass is mown,
do we really hear them,
when we lift the phone.

Of course we can
you know it's true
our spirit friends are with us
in everything we do.

P McGilloway

FLOWERS OF REMEMBRANCE

Happy I was till I saw you,
Red, and white, and pink, and blue.
You fell from my hand
And covered the ground,
Until you stretched
For miles around.
You covered my head
And entered my mind,
Discovering memories
I'd sought to leave behind.
A tender touch, a loving smile,
A vision not seen for a while.
I turned my head, I must be free,
But there again, you're here with me,
Holding me close, whispering my name,
Reassuring me, over and over again.
Of your tender love,
Your tender care.
Suddenly - gone - you're not there.
I must remain, I may not follow you,
I place these flowers of brilliant hue
Lovingly, upon your grave.
Goodbye, goodbye,
I miss you.

Elizabeth Birch

FIFTY PLUS

Looking back along the track
At things you might have done
Wasted opportunities
More love to give, another son

Rewind the hands of time
But make the same mistakes
Hard to live with failure
Still don't recognise the breaks

So time goes on and soon
The sun begins to fade
But not the pain
Look to share the life you've made

And no one wants it anymore
I doubt they ever did
And so you die
But did you ever really live

V Elmer

AS I LOOKED OUT OF MY WINDOW

As I looked out of my steamy window and saw the crisp snow lying on the ground,
As I looked up into the starry sky I saw the flaky snow falling around.
As I felt the warmth of my coal fire just resting on my cheeks,
I stole a thought and remembered how my loved grandpa sleeps.
Why can't he be right next to me feeling the warmth of my fire?
But then I realised he's here no more, he's gone to things much higher.
So as I looked out of my window and saw that the icy snow had settled on the ground,
I smiled because I know that when my head touches my pillow tonight
I'll sleep safe and sound.

Leonnie R

REFLECTIONS OF MY CHILDHOOD

When I look back on my childhood,
they were days of happiness.
Even though the world was at war,
we never knew much distress.

Clothes and food were all rationed,
I didn't have many toys.
Our parents had to make do and mend,
yet Christmas still held many joys.

I recall my school summer holidays,
when to the seaside we would go.
Frolicking under a summer sun,
Days so wonderful to know.

Growing up was a pleasant pastime,
for the future that lay ahead.
Learning all about life's problems,
didn't fill me with dread.

I never thought about getting older,
knew childhood wouldn't be the same.
And now that I am middle aged,
I would love to be young again.

Jim Roberts

THE RETURN

The air grew colder, and the woman's face
Contorted suddenly, lost all its grace
And beauty. But then from her mouth issued
A piercing scream. After that, like tissue
Just floating in a stream, it formed itself
Into a child. She gazed around herself,
Then cried out 'Mother.' Held her arms out wide.

Amanda Howse

A PEDLAR OF DREAMS

When I was a child
he'd come down the street
With his horse and his cart -
Old shoes on his feet.

His cry would be raucous -
'Old rags and old bones' -
What a clatter he'd make
On the rough cobblestones.

Then out they'd come rushing
The girls and the boys,
Screaming and shouting -
They'd make such a noise
so eager they were
For one of his toys.

Balloons were the favourite -
And upward they'd fly
A riot of colour
To transform the sky
And change a world
That was drab and grey
With magical colours
Just for a day.

Then the horse would grow restive
And stamp his feet
And the ragged old man
would start down the street.
His clothes were so shabby
But I watched and he seemed
Not a ragged old man
But a pedlar of dreams.

Margaret Parry

DEATH

Death is a cruel hard joke
Which is beyond understanding.
It leaves in its wake
Destruction, grief and little hope for
the onward journey.

Death is not a friend.
it is the one who steals from us,
Leaving behind a path filled with
Loss and unhappiness.

Death can arrive
At anytime it chooses.
Quite often unexpected and
Always with devastating results.

Death is a cruel hard joke
Which is beyond understanding.
Its road is followed closely by
Feelings of loss, sadness and despair.

Debbie Benton

REGRETS

Sometimes I wish I could turn the clock back
That I could have my former years
Then I would make an effort to console
The many children who this day live in fear
I'd like to cradle them with love
To show we really care
Give them hope and comfort whatever they may bear
Alas I am no longer young but my heart is warm and true
And every day that dawns for me
I'll say a prayer for you

Christine Ferguson

GRANDMA REMEMBERS

What no electric! My grandchild said,
No a candle lit me to my bed,
How did we manage you may think
When we had no tap or kitchen sink,
Water was drawn from pump or well,
Carried home in a bucket, I can tell,

Cooking was done on a kitchen range,
With wood and coal, which may sound strange,
All had to be carried, so much work,
And such a lot of dust and dirt,
But although there was so much to do,
Sometimes my dears I pity you,

You see it was such a joy to be,
Around the fire as a family,
With potatoes in the oven roasting,
Thick bread on long forks a-toasting,
Granny and Granddad were never in the way,
No one would want them there today,

To tell us tales of days before,
Of work in fields and times of war,
There was no need of doors to lock,
Neighbours dropped in without a knock,
To lend a hand, when times were bad,
Or to share our joy when we were glad,

We never knew the fear of mugging,
But of family love and lots of hugging,
It was a time of being together,
A time I fear has gone forever.

Rhoda Woodward

ANNIVERSARY

It was our 40th, some days ago,
Did you remember, wherever you are?
I sat alone and wished you well,
Hoping my dreams would stretch that far.

I went to our special place that day,
And smiled at my memory:
A dancing you with golden hair,
A sapphire sky, a younger me.

I remembered when I took your hand,
And knelt before your sparkling eyes . . .
How was I to know that God was cruel?
How was I to know He spoke such lies?

I went to visit your ageing grave,
Hidden in the shadows, buried in the dirt,
I laid flowers and tears came to my eyes,
I saw your face with a tearing hurt.

And so I went back to our house -
So still and silent I could've been dead -
All that I thought of at the time,
Was 'I love you, I love you' chasing round in my head.

It was my 60th some days ago,
Did you remember, wherever you are?
I sat alone and wished for death,
Wanting to go where I'd been barred.

K Gribble

MY MEMORY BOOK

In solitude I open my memory book,
Turning the pages, what do I see?
On every page, wherever I look,
Treasured memories, come flooding back to me.

Of school days, and the lessons we learnt,
The fun we all had, games we all played.
When we had done well, the praise we earnt,
But when we misbehaved, boy! Then we paid.

Those teenage years, and the remembered song,
Snappy suits and Brylcream hair.
Chasing the girls, but never doing wrong,
We were the lads, the devil may care.

Then the world became a place of strife,
And in some way, we all played our part.
But sadly, many a good friend left this life,
The rest came back to make a fresh start.

We all then went our different ways,
Single or married, our lives to pursue.
Wife or friend to share our days,
To our earlier life, a sad adieu.

Time has now passed, the years rolled by,
Childhood, youth and manhood too.
Before I close my book and sigh,
I'll relive the memories and try not to cry.

Les Reeves

SADLY

Whene'er I look back
On days started, then done,
I remember good people
Who've been and have gone.
I think with regret
Of the folks once I knew.
Of my friends fast becoming
Increasingly few.
'Tis then that I look
In the glass on the wall,
And I say to myself,
'You're not ageing at all'
But all of a sudden
The wind blows real cold,
For I know in my heart
I am growing quite old.
And I sadly note then
That the hour newly passed,
Is another one near
To my own very last.

Dorothy Hitchman

MEMORIES

Wen ha climbs owt o' bed an' th' curtains hal draw
Jus to si wot day an wether as I' store
An it's then wen tha noas as thart gerring owld
Wen all o' thi' body it shivers wi' cowld.

It gets thi to thinking o' winters long past
Wen snow an sledgin fer weeks seemed to last
It ne're seem'd slushy nor coloured dark grey
But as white as all the memories of a childhood day.

Wid roll giant snowballs from top o'th hill
Then to build us a snowman wid set to wi' a will
Wi' coals fer its eyes an' a hat on its head
It'd hold our attention till it were time fer bed.

Perhaps it's as well that these memories of mine
Have become somewhat tinted with the passage of time
No mention of toes that were frozen with cold
But that's one of the advantages you get when you're old.

Steven Parker

LIFE'S MEMORIES

They can be good, they can be bad,
These memories of mine,
Sometimes happy, sometimes sad
Pictures from the past
Like slides on a screen, reliving emotions
Just what do they mean?
You can live on memories for all your life long
Or live life to the full,
Make your memories, make you strong
Think positive, not negative throughout all your life.
For memories serve a purpose if you don't want toil and strife
They make you remember what you didn't do right.
With a thought, word or deed, when you wanted to fight
You sometimes learn life's lessons
From the bad times you know,
So learn from your life's memories,
Then onward, your soul can grow.

Carol Ann Pritchard

IN THE OLD DAYS

When cobbled streets were lit by gas lamps,
and outhouses lined the back lanes.
The family would huddle in front of the hearth,
looking for pictures in coals and the flames.

The smell of baked bread would flow from the house
and welcome all who would venture within.
The front step was scrubbed every morning,
before filling dad's bath of cold tin.

Men in the pub would play cards till the bell,
rolling their own with tobacco they'd bought.
Then home they would sway, as they strolled arm in arm,
to remember the war and their comrades who'd fought.

At a time when doors were left open,
when neighbours would share and stand strong.
They had fought the good fight for the living,
so, in England we would all still belong.

When the door opened he would enter,
and lay his cloth cap on the chair.
He'd glance at his uniformed picture,
as he ran fingers through now thinning hair.

Making his way to the staircase,
he turned and paused for a while,
thinking thoughts of the future,
he gingerly rendered a smile.

Susan Richardsen

VE DAY MEMORIES

I watch you as your standing there
As you look in the window
I wonder what memories go flooding
Through your mind

Old photos of people cheering on Victory Day
Mementoes lying there, now seem a lifetime away
An old war map a ration book, at these things
I see you look

50 years ago today you were celebrating VE day

A time to remember long lost friends, and
Those who died. You remember with great pride.
I wonder what you are feeling there inside.

For a fleeting moment I thought I could see
That brave young man, that gave his youth
For me.

I want to thank him as I watch him there
And in his memories I would like to share.
But an intrusion I know I would be, so I'll
Leave him to his memories.

I feel a tear upon my cheek, and I know if
Only I would dare to speak, I would say
Thank you my friend for what you did, and to
all your friends who died for us,
I know mere words are not enough.

So I'll stand here in silence, and watch
You go by, and I'll say a silent thank you and
A silent goodbye.

May Strike

SHADOWS IN THE STREET

Shattered glass,
Broken hearts,
Tears of pain and laughter.

Droning engines,
Heavy boots,
Men scurrying after.

Silent tongues,
Strange fears,
Shadows in the street.

Cold metal,
Empty chamber,
Success or defeat.

Sudden thud,
Hellish yell,
Drifting to an after life.

Memories are
all that's left
for a heart that burns an eternal light.

Anton Scullion

NORFOLK REVISITED

Back to memory vividly - bold,
a walk by the cornfields of harvested gold.

War announced to all the world
that Sunday morning, the news unfurled.
Sad goodbyes and tears were shed,
sirens called us, from our beds.

'It won't be long - can't land at Dover'
'You wait and see - get Christmas over!'
Fierce battles rage o'er land, sea, and air
fragile the promises, devastation, despair.

Survived we these our desperate times,
Peace again, returned these climes.
Bells in steeples praises pealed,
loved ones returned, reliance healed.

Eric Mason

MIDDLETON MEMORIES

The gardens where I used to sit and eat ice-cream from Meggetts
Have long since been replaced by the Arndale shopping centre.
My infant school at Durnford Street, no more there can I venture.
The Long Street Parish School became a restaurant with *inside* toilets.
The grammar school in Rectory Street is now a pile of rubble
'You must wear your green berets or you will be in trouble,'
The market, too, has changed its site, the town hall made more modern
The bandstand in the park has made me reminisce and ponder.
The concerts at the Co-op hall both classical and pop
And Middy baths - the place to go for the Christmas Eve hop.
Sledging down from Alki Hall towards the river Irk,
Blackberrying in Hopwood Clough before it got too dark.
The Empire and the Victory (or 'flea-pit' as known by some)
Tommy's field off the Old Road where the fairground made its home.
Town planners try to change its looks but memories are there
I'm proud to say I was born and bred a Middleton Moonraker.

J Davis

BOGGART OF THE CLOUGH

We used to visit Boggart Hole Clough when I was just a lad.
How this park came by its strange name, one day I asked my dad.
He told me once a farmer lived in the bottom of the clough.
The boggart was a mischievous sprite, and one day, sure enough,
he moved in with the family and made himself at home
and then the ghostly visitor all sorts of tricks performed,
like stripping bedclothes off the bed, and tapping on the door,
or sending pots and pans and dishes clattering on the floor.
At dead of night his shrieks of impish laughter rent the air;
he terrified the children with loud footsteps on the stairs.
he'd snatch the bread and butter from the little baby's plate,
and workmen, afraid to come inside, would linger by the gate.
At last the poor farmer and his wife could stand no more of it,
deciding that their only course of action was to flit.
'We'll pack up everything,' they said, 'and move to another farm.
If we can leave the boggart behind, he'll do us no more harm.'
So with a wagon piled high with all their household stuff,
they travelled on rejoicing till they'd almost left the clough,
when the boggart's evil voice was heard inside an empty churn:
'I've flitted with you!'
'What?' said the farmer, 'then we will return.'
And so the farmer's family to their former home went back.
I wonder if the boggart laughed and helped them to unpack?
They say they all lived peacefully together from that day,
And no-one's seen the boggart since - I looked again today.

Alan Smith

OLD LANCASHIRE

Long gone are the clogs and shawl
The dark satanic mills and all
The deep dark pits are no more
Where young children had to work by the score
Long gone the old Lamplighter with his long hooked stick
The clatter of clogs every morning at six
Gone are the horsedrawn carts delivering milk and coal
Sad was the time with so many men on the dole
As a small child I could not understand, why my father had work to be at
While the men up the road, stood around in groups,
with nothing to do, but chat
I did not know how lucky I was, for they had only a few shillings
a week to do all, but get fat!

Long gone and almost forgotten now, are those dark dreary days
Perhaps it's as well for they were long and hard in so many ways
There was no easy way to lighten the load,
How my mother longed for a garden, bright with flowers of every hue
She so hated the grey backyard with the bricks and the outside loo
Where as I remember, creepy crawly spiders usually accompanied you!

Mostly Lancashire is thought of as damp and cold
But not the folks, or so we are told
Friendly and kind we like to be
With always a warm welcome, and a nice cup of tea
It does rain quite a lot, but there are lovely places to be
Where else will you find the trees and the grass always so very green to see?

Very few now will remember those days
For it is almost a century ago
How things have changed so
I wonder what it will be like, the next generation to know?
Probably visiting the moon will be quite natural to go!

Edna Parrington

JAMIE

I gaze from my window and capture the sight
A little boy playing, with joy and delight.
His laughter and smiles just for me they belong . . .
What comfort he brings now his daddy has gone.

O Jamie, sweet Jamie, my pride and my joy
Heaven has sent you - my own baby boy.
I'll love you forever - I will till I die,
Till the birds still their singing . . .
And the rivers run dry.

He stands at the altar on his wedding day
So happy and proud, as he kneels there to pray.
The tears fill my eyes when I think of the span,
How fast he has grown from a boy to a man.

Now the years have gone by and my dreams have come true.
Memories of old are rekindled anew . . .
With his hand in mine a new life has begun.
What wonder he brings to me . . . my Jamie's son.

F MacDougall

WHERE GOES THE TIME

Where goes the time that passes by,
absorbed by land, by sea, by sky.
Where goes the time that is no more,
lost to the night that was before.
Where goes the joy, the pain, the tears,
meshed with 'ago's' and 'yesteryears'.
Where goes the childhood we once held,
lost to nostalgia and memories quelled.

Where goes the time that passes by,
the time that elapses the time that flies.
Where goes the day and night that part,
lost to tomorrow but locked in our hearts.

Julie Howard

THE PIT

When I was a lad, in Lancs,
Most boys - they went down the mine,
Where it was always the night,
And you never saw the sun shine.

Dad said 'Get the-sell down to the pit-face,
And earn us a few extra bob.'
I didn't fancy it very much,
But I had to have some kind of job.

What a fright, when I went down the lift shaft,
And then lost sight of the top.
By the time we got to the bottom,
They needed a bucket and mop!

They put me to work at the coal-face,
I was black from my head to my toes,
And all that flippin' coal dust,
Went up everywhere - even my nose!

I think I lasted a fortnight,
And didn't enjoy it one bit,
I can't say that I have fond memories,
When recalling my time down the pit.

M L Bond

CHILDHOOD MEMORIES

On a farm I spent my early years
No violence there, no doubts or fears
Down to the farm a rough stone track
No concrete for us, no tarmac
In the kitchen a large stone sink
With an old brass tap to have a drink
Stone slab floors, all scrubbed white
An oil lamp or candle for a light
Bedroom windows thick with ice
Get undressed in a trice
A hot water bottle, a soft feather bed
Above it an iron and brass bedhead
First thing in the morning light the fire
Suspend the kettle on a piece of wire
Fill up the boiler to get the water hot
Make up the fire it must heat the lot
Frying pan on there are men to be fed
Bacon, eggs and crisp fried bread
Time for toast when the fire glows red
A long wire fork to spear the bread
Take out the damper, it cannot stay
The oven must be hot for baking today
Dough on the hearth left to rise
Next it has to be cut to size
Placed in loaf tins left to rest
Baked till done a tap was the test
Next came oatcakes, cakes and pies
Good that's the lot Grandma sighs.
But the smell lingered on, I can smell it yet
These are things I can never forget.

Jean Thornton

LOOKING BACK

Looking back to Lancashire,
As I knew it in the twenties,
It makes the poverty of today
Seem like the 'Land of Plenty'.

And yet the pilferings that we had
Were few and far between.
No beating up the old folks
By youngsters in their teens.

Young girls were safe to walk the streets,
Not like it is today.
People gave a helping hand,
And helped folk on their way.

We all were in the same old boat,
No holidays overseas.
A day at Blackpool, once a year
Was the best we could achieve.

And yet we found our happiness
In simple little pleasures.
Our Friday penny from our Dad
Was as good as hidden treasure.

Why can't we be like that today?
Take life for what it's worth
We've got our lovely Lancashire
Why should we want the Earth?

Olive Smith

YOUNG DREAMS OF DERBY

If all my dreams, in childhood,
Could all come true again.
One that gave me quite a thrill
Was building a secret den.
With corrugated sheeting, rusting at the edges,
Bits of timber and old rope, even parts of hedges.
We'd crowd inside, when all was done,
And live a childhood dream,
Of sultans, treasures, palaces,
And dishes of ice-cream.
The old 'Brickyard' was hilly clay,
With rubbish tipped where we would play.
But our own adventure playground
With dreams to stage and play.
There were old kilns looking like derelict caverns
And a chimney really tall.
They demolished them on one fine day,
I didn't see them fall.

Eventually it was all filled in
And grassed to make it green.
With tarmac, smoothed in ribboned strips,
And here and there some trees.
All the terraced houses were raised unto the ground
And families were moved away,
Most neighbours outward bound.
Along came builders by the score
With sandy coloured bricks,
They built houses and a nursery school,
It happened, oh so quick.
My young dreams of Derby
Seemed to distance with the past.
The years rushed by so rapidly
But the memories, they still last.

S J Southall

LOSING MY MEMORY . . .

I think I have been here years,
it must be such a long time,
just how long I cannot tell,
I have lost the grasp of what time is.

In the beginning,
when I arrived,
as much as I remember.

I shovelled piles of dust into rows of seven,
in lines, to tell,
but the dust just blew away,
and now I cannot count to seven,
I cannot imagine its shape or name.

It's black here all the time,
like the nothingness in my head,
grew too big and escaped outside,
I let it grow what could I do?

I lapse sometimes, sleep I think,
a gap to separate blocks of nothing,
aware, then not aware.

Maybe there is no gap, a decent interval,
between awake and not awake,
maybe it's so quick it just appears I sit here blinking,

Stepping to one side of myself,
I can see what it's all been for,
as the last piece of black escapes my head,
in the blink of an eye . . .

Liza Hunter

LOOKING BACK AND LOOKING FORWARD

He was just my father-in-law
But as dear as a dad to me
In him the help and the love I saw
Was as dear as dear could be.

His Saviour meant a lot to him
And I'm sure he means more now
For in his presence without a sin
He with sincerity will bow.

On that sad morn his last words to Gran
Were as if in his mind he doubted
'If they don't bow the knee in time
they will in eternity' he shouted.

In that small Newcastle town
While on earth he loved to be
There the famous Mountains of Mourne
Sweep down to the deep blue sea.

He spent many a happy hour
Out in that loved Irish Sea
Where he would go on a fishing tour
And would be as happy as could be.

His small granddaughter was asked in church one day
'Tell me is your Pop in this place?'
She answered with worlds of dismay
'He's the one with the smiling face.'

Gran and us on our journey here
Will keep looking for that heavenly shore
For we will all meet there
Never to part no more.

Maureen Dawson

TOO QUICK

It's gone too quick
The years before.
Now age is knocking
At the door.
Memories of happy days
Are sought to keep
the pain at bay
That youth and love
have passed away
And loneliness is ready to
land upon fresh pastures new.

It's gone too quick
Youthful fun and laughter,
And the promises
Of happy ever after
That sprang from blissful
innocence of youth
Maturing into motherhood.
The special years
With precious hours
That couldn't hold back
time's passing power.

Now I'm older
What does the future
hold for me?
Fulfilment in grace?
Or inadequacy?

June Rampton

MEMORIES

When you were little you played with your toys
People would stop us and praise you four boys
The noise it seemed endless the breakages worse
Toys food and clothing stretched wallet and purse
Time flew by quickly it seemed almost in haste
To bring you to teen years growing apace.

Now came the music thumping and loud
And telephone calls with bills in the cloud
Your car out of petrol the problem is ours
As we came to collect you at late pm hours.

Then came the first time you stayed out all night
And Dad toured the town to see if you're alright
We sat up and worried as if you were small
You came home at am no worries at all
Now you are gone to a house of your own
We smile and remember pleased that you've grown.

Jane Darnell

FOREVER YOUNG

Little girl keeping her head high,
Runs through the fields so summer sweet,
Her laughter reaches the depths of the sky,
Buttercups dancing around her feet,

The cherished memories of childhood,
A smile which is frozen in time,
When once everything felt so very good,
When life is at its prime.

So little girl don't grow so fast,
You'll miss it when it's gone,
The magical dreams which seemed to last,
Won't stay for ever long.

Lisa Forni

THE VILLAGE GREEN

When I was very young
I saw a wondrous sight.
Fairies, elfins, small animals,
Dancing on the village green,
In the bright moonlight.
As the years have rolled by,
I have witnessed their dancing -
Many times, and that's no lie.
Then suddenly they went away.
I know not why.
I've often wondered what
Became of them, did they die?
Until my great-granddaughter
Came to stay,
One night she climbed into my bed,
And whispered in my ear, Great Nan-na
I've seen a magic sight, I've seen
Fairies, and small animals dancing
In the bright moonlight.
I was so happy they had returned
To give pleasure to my descendant -
A lovely little girl.
I hope they will stay for many a year
As time runs out for this old dear.
Soon I will be 104, so I'll say goodnight,
God bless, as I close my front door.

Gordon Dangerfield

A NORFOLK BOY - EDWARD JAMES TUTTLE

Edward James was born
Back in 1895
In Mattishall in Norfolk
He was glad to be alive.

Victoria was the queen then
Approaching her Jubilee
Edward went to school each day
From nine 'til half past three.

And then schooldays were over
He worked for Mr Neave
Who owned the village grocer's shop
Selling things from morn 'til eve.

When the Great War started
Edward felt so brave
He enlisted with the Norfolks
But was bound for an early grave.

He wanted to see action
To fight the wicked foe
So joined the Essex regiment
Who were up and ready to go.

The ship the *Royal Edward*
Was bound for Gallipoli
He sailed away at eight o'clock
Over the bright blue sea.

The torpedo it struck quickly
In the Aegean Sea
Men and horses all went down
There was nothing left to be.

Postscript:

He died in 1915
His is an unmarked grave
His name is on a memorial
At Cape Helles - far away.

Valerie Tuttle

LIKE THINGS USED TO BE

Tiny little houses - smoking chimneys,
whitewashed steps - brass knockers.
The muffin man - a tray on his head
shouting enough to waken the dead.
The tallyman - clothing on tick,
and the lamplighter doing his rounds.
Rag and bone man with pony and cart,
'I'll have that tin bath for a start'
Dad back from the Labour Exchange,
no jobs about - no money either;
not even for a glass of cider.
Rent man calls - 'Please call next week'
he reckons we've got a ruddy cheek.
Father just glares and dear mother frowns
as we dress for school in hand me downs.
Our Tommy has joined the Army now
and all for a few shillings pay;
but anything's better than this
at least he can eat every day.

David T Wicking

TRANQUILLITY SHATTERED

The sirens howled, the bombs whistled down,
Huge fires raged across Coventry town,
Everyone ran out of the theatre, showing, 'Gone with the Wind',
Then it fell to ashes, bombed to the ground,
One fell on our shelter, right on the top,
But we were truly blessed, it did not go off,
Rubbing my eyes, while Mother was urgently calling, and half asleep,
I jumped into my little red siren suit and zipped up the front with a squeak,
Clutching my red Mickey Mouse gasmask, I ran down the stairs,
And across the exploding flashing garden, where once I had played,
Dad hitch-hiked on a fire engine all the way to London,
To put the story in the papers that Coventry was a cauldron,
Mum lost her ration book which we found years later,
Dropped down the back of the wooden mantelpiece, what a disaster,
Dad joined the army, a last photo was taken,
I sat on his knee, my brother wore his army cap, this picture was never to be forgotten,
Dad trained many soldiers who never came back,
He took his typewriter across the desert, he was a true desert rat,
Suddenly the war was over, the sun peeped out again,
To Coventry station to welcome him home, the whole family ran,
Never will I forget that magic moment as he stepped off the train,
Crushing and kissing Mum, and the family, till we were breathless from his squeezing crushing frame,
All the soldiers were whistling and watching him, he didn't give a hang,
He was home at last from the clutches of Hitler Satan,
Uncle Harold reached his front door, a starving emaciated skeleton,
He had to be weaned on bread and milk for weeks before he could eat anything,
Auntie Mabel sat in the bath her curlers still in her hair,
And she had wanted to look so nice when he arrived there,
He walked from Dunkirk to Germany, from happiness to Hell and back,
Bombs, fires and sirens, our memories are buried in the ashes!

Pauline Starr

THE BLUE COUNTESS

Some quarrymen died working the slate
Out in all the weather
Sometimes the dust, sometimes the blast
Left a family without a provider.

No work no pay - so they struggled on
Through winter's rain and chill
For just a pittance at the end of the week
Hard work on the side of the hill.

With knotted fingers cut on the slate
And back bowed against the wind
Men of the quarries had to be strong
To do the work they did.

The ladies stacked up row by row.
Cost many strong men their pride
These men indeed were the lucky ones
For many a quarryman died.

The Duchess Fach and the Duchess Fawr
These were always dressed with care
Quarrymen sang doing their work
But now there's no-one there.

Now the galleries spend their quiet days
No blasts at ten and three
Rusting trucks are all that's left
Reminding you and me.

We should remember how our fathers lived
A bygone age now dead
Remember too the fun we had
Remember out heritage.

Gaerwyn Williams

BRIDGE OF TIME

I stood on a bridge familiar and I was a child again
As the memories flooded back of days where I would remain.
My mind flew back to the farmhouse and my own little room therein
Where I listened to the birdsong and the farmyard's cheery din.
The schoolhouse, now a cottage, with gardens beautifully laid,
Yet there in my childhood memories I could see the desks again.
And the little church still waiting for any to enter inside,
Cool, and peacefully sounding the bells at eventide.
Oft in my childhood ventures I walked down the country lanes
Mid the amber colours of autumn, or touched by the soft spring rains.
And summers seemed never ending amid the bright cornfields' gold,
With all the many treasures the countryside can hold:
The wayside flowers sweetly peeping beneath the hedgerows of bramble,
The clip clop of a horse's hooves, and the joy of a country ramble.
The bridge holds many memories where friends would gather and meet,
There in the flowing river we would paddle our dusty feet.
And then to watch the blacksmith we would stand for many an hour
No greater thrill for any child than the smithy's mighty power.
Although there have been some changes, for fifty years have passed by
The village is still a treasure I would rest in when I die.
And the bridge across the river spans my memories of the years
Where I spent my happy childhood, remembered now with tears.

Joan Heybourn

MY PONY

Gone are the long and endless days,
We shared, in the summer haze.
You shared my life, my childhood years,
I told you my secrets and my fears.
The memories of times gone by,
Brings a tear to my eye.

As I remember the roads we travelled,
Muddled thoughts, become unravelled.
I see us now together again,
Riding down some country lane.
My childhood pal and my best friend,
How I wish we could ride together again.

Hazel Jackson

REMEMBERING

Starting the day was always fine
That is if you got up in time.
'Hurry,' said mum we'll miss the bus
I remember breakfast was such a rush.

Then on to school where playtime was fun
Skipping, marbles, just enjoying the sun.
Reading comics like Girl and School Friend
Eating sherbet fountains, that was the trend.

Home from school, still work to be done
Sums and writing, exams to be won.
Then half an hour playing in the street
Knock down ginger, we were quick on our feet.

Then mum called us in, 'Get ready for bed,'
We didn't argue with what she said
Because we had pillow fights at night
As soon as she turned off the light.

And as we remember our times as a child
Some happenings are quite beguiled,
So I think it's fair to say without fear
Nothing compares with yesteryear.

Yvonne M Wiseman

YESTERDAYS

When I was just a little girl
My horizons yet to broaden
I lived amid the dirt and grime
Of a colliery place called Horden
Coal dust was familiar
'Pit clothes' working gear
The coal our fathers' livelihood
To some brought many a tear
The dangerous occupation
So many took for granted
Fuelled smoky fires in terraced rows
Where never a tree was planted

Our playground was the dusty street
Or cement of the backyard
Yet life seemed satisfying then
So we didn't think it hard
In chapel on the Sabbath
We wore our Sunday best
As in those days the seventh day
Remained a day of rest

If we'd thought about security
As we have to in these days
The changes between then and now
Truly would amaze
We did know about contentment
And could wander without fear
The simple poor?
No we were rich
In those days of yesteryear.

Jeannette Facchini

CHILDHOOD GAMES

Before the days of television came to our valley town,
We children played very simple games
And I thought I would write some down.
Skipping of course was a popular game
Where we could show off our skill,
But many times we tripped and fell
When 'showing-off' down a hill.
We played hopscotch on the road
As very little traffic came our way.
With chalk we would draw on the ground
And each had their own stone to play.
Whip and top was a fun game
Specially when we found,
That by chalking coloured patterns
On the tops they looked pretty going round.
There were many ball games,
In 'Fivesy' you threw one against a wall,
Then did some clever footwork catching it
Before it could fall.
Bowling a hoop along the road,
Swinging from a lamp-post on a rope.
Dancing in a circle singing songs,
With a clay pipe blowing bubbles
Made from water and soap.
Our imaginations had no bounds -
Boredom we never knew.
These were the happy pleasant days
In which we children grew.

Marian Such

UNTITLED

When he was a lad parents so poor
Everyone hung their key on a string on the door.
Holes in his socks, holes in his shoes
Tin baths in living room, outside loos,
Cod Liver oil, dripping on bread
Nits in your hair, nits in your bed
Done what you're told, done what was said
Coal fires, lino, long walks to school
Kids in short trousers, acting the fool
Lads behind bike sheds rolling a fag
Lads and lassies queuing up for a drag.

Headmaster, teachers, horrible cooks,
Frog-spawn, lumpy custard and pie.
A smack with a ruler, a poke in the eye
A ride on a trolley bus without any fuss
A tram ride to Stratford, a walk to Bow
Mum and dad shopping down Club Row
Pianos in pubs sawdust on floors
No need for bouncers on those doors.

Conkers and kites, derelict houses, bomb sites
Saturday morning pictures Snowy and Jock
Sing to the organ, Southend rock
Steam trains, hop picking, dockers with hooks
Lads dressed up in their Sunday best
Brother's shirts, their cousin's vests.
Singing in Sunday school looking your best
A clip round the ear for being a pest
Rag and Bone men horses and carts
Lads and lassies had a hard time then.

Jean Spearing

PROPER MONEY

I remember D-Day well.
Not those famed landings in Normandy,
but the day they changed the currency.
Our monetary system was cast aside
and all the prices were decimalised.
Items were more expensive to sell
Oh yes. I remember D-Day well.

Once, there were ha'pennies I had gained
I saw them crushed by a passing train.
Pennies were a kind of coppery brown,
took me for a ride on a trolley to town.
Threepenny bits were given away
each Sunday on a collection tray.
All these fine coins dismissed without thanks
into our past and memory banks.

And what a waste all that schooling proved,
to learn LSD then have it removed.
To be taught in the method of shillings and florins
just as we were Shakespeare and William of Orange.
They took our sixpences without permission
with some of them still in mint condition.

Much water has flown under bridges since then,
these days it's all done in multiples of ten.
Today's modern youngsters don't give a thought
as to what three and fourpence might once have bought.
And their calculations wouldn't be done in a hurry
if only they still had to use proper money.
A young mathematician's unrivalled hell,
Oh yes, I remember D-Day quite well.

Keith Jenkinson

MAM AND DAD

Do you remember
a long time ago
when into this world I came?
You gave me a life
through your love for each other
then thoughtfully gave me my name.

And so from a baby
you nursed me through life
teaching me both, good and bad.
I learned that when help or advice
I may need
I had only to ask Mam and Dad

But then
as I grew to an adult
I caused you such sorrow and pain.
The worry you suffered
the anger and doubt
makes me now feel so very ashamed.

So now I have grown up and married
and have started a life of my own
I want you to know
that your own little girl
will never stop loving you so.
She will never be able to tell you
how thankful she is that you two
have always cared so much about her
that's why she cares so much
for you.

Ruth Thomas

WHEN I WAS A LASS . . . OH BRADDA HEAD!

To the beautiful Isle of Man I sailed
Just sixty four years ago
'Twas the maiden voyage of the New Lady of Man
On her I was fortunate to go
A nurse-maid was I - just fifteen years old
This sail should have been such a pleasure
My wealthy employers were given a tour
I was included in all without measure
Yet though I knew it was my lucky break
My feelings were so uncanny
If I could only understand
Why feelings like this I should carry?
Our destination was Port Erin
We landed safely there
Maybe it is imagination I thought
Though mystery was still in the air.
I took the children to Bradda Head
I stood looking out to sea
Suddenly my answer came
If only back home I could be
In good health was mum when I left her
Yet the answer I got was so startling
I knew my dear mum was going to die
Please God not my last parting
Eight weeks I worked so uneasy
Should she die before I reached home
Yet home I went and there she was
But in six weeks we had lost our mum
Oh Bradda Head! Oh Bradda Head!
How I have remembered you!

Annie Davies

OUR ANNIVERSARY

Thirty years ago today
Haven't we done swell?
Since we exchanged our wedding vows
St Stephen's Church, (?) ...well

Marriages are made in heaven they say,
Now I know that's true
For it sure was a lucky day
For me when I met and married you.

So we started out in life
Yes we married young.
About one year later
we had a little son.

Two fine daughters followed
and though that's not unique,
holding on to little hands
made our lives complete.

So we made our way through life
Children all have grown.
For now our son is married with a
youngster of his own.

Silence reigns in our house now
Oh how time has flown.
Children are all settled
with full lives of their own.

But though we're getting older
don't let's fret or frown
I still ready *fairy stories*
and you still *clown around.*

Did I say our house was quiet?
Oh no that cannot be.
There's much fun joy and laughter
Our grandson's come for tea!

F Milsom

NO-ONE FEARED THE SHADOWS THEN

At the tender age of eight or nine
Happily, I played
In the street both night and day,
No need to be afraid.

With my friends till ten at night
The streets were safe and free,
Jumping hedges, trick or treat
No danger threatened me.

Summer nights of fun were spent
Beneath the moonlit sky,
No-one feared the shadows then
And no-one pondered why.

Fifteen years have seen such change
Now streets are out of bounds,
Laughter no more fills the air
Above the playing grounds.

Every day a child's at risk
Of being snatched away,
What happened to those carefree days
When I went out to play?

Sarah Maycock

MY CHILDHOOD HOME

I remember cherry blossom swaying in the breeze,
And miniature golf on the lawn,
Loganberries fresh picked for our teas,
And a blackbird's clear song in the morn.

The smell of coffee fresh percolating on the stove,
Mint sauce being chopped for lunch,
Bumble bees that endlessly did rove
Around blue delphiniums in a bunch.

The bird-stand where greedy starlings constantly did fight,
Arched mauve clematis that I'd pass,
An incinerator we did light,
To burn green hedge cuttings and dead grass.

Lily of the Valley growing densely by the fence,
The shade of the mauve lilac tree,
Giant crimson dahlias with heads immense,
Yellow luscious pears for all to see.

Constant music from the piano, my aunt did play,
Some latest songs that we all sang.
A grandfather clock that chimed all day,
The doorbell that the many guests rang.

An oak dresser adorned with willow-patterned plates,
Tables with dress patterns cut out,
On top of the sideboard home-made cakes,
There were two old cats that laid about.

My childhood home with so many pleasant memories -
It was my second home to be.
For I was orphaned at eight years' old,
My aunt and uncle adopted me.

G A Burgess

JENNIFER

Don't think of me with sadness
Remember me and smile,
For we are all but flowers
That bloom for just a while.

If I brought you happiness
Then remember me with joy,
For we are but the summer
Sunshine, just a golden toy

If I brought you heartache,
At times I know I must,
Then remember all the good times
For we are all but dust.

I know you dream of golden days
When you just beamed with pride
As people fussed and cuddled me
As I stood by your side.

So I will live forever
In everything you do,
I will never leave you
Because I loved you too.

I'm your beloved Jennifer
Remember me that way,
For I am only sleeping
'Til we meet again one day.

Jaqui Coleman

THE FORGOTTEN CHURCHYARD

The churchyard is deserted,
Overgrown with weeds,
It looks so desolate, so dark,
Amongst foreboding trees.

Very old, great and small,
Death has come to one and all,
The lord and lady in their tomb,
And nearby lies a humble groom.

Husband, wife, lover, friend,
How did they toil?
Now it's only bones that lay,
Beneath the cold dark soil.

Some were given a pauper's grave,
Whose remains lie where?
So many died in early years,
Was theirs a life of care?

The nobleman lies, the poor man near,
No longer master, servant here,
Innkeeper, carpenter, blacksmith, maid,
Now they all at rest are laid.

Not many lived till forty,
No great age at all,
And all that's left, a stone,
Propped against a wall.

Inscriptions faded weather-worn,
Overgrown by bramble, thorn,
No flowers placed with loving care,
Only grass and nettles there.

Margaret Ann Thompson

THE TARMAC SNAKE

Do you remember the old horse-chestnut
That stands at the heart of our town
Which graced the railway station,
When the trains ran up and down?

Did you search the ground for conkers,
In the shade cast deep from its bough?
Which sheltered us as children,
And we must shelter now.

Would you like the snake of tarmac,
To slide across our green
And take away forever
The beauty of this scene?

More than a fight for the life of a tree -
More than a cry from the town -
But a plea for the peace and tranquillity,
That will cease if the tree is cut down.

Tired of the phrase 'It does seem a shame,'
It's time that we all made a stand,
Let us object, not share in the blame,
For destroying the green of our land!

Something old, something new; this is not the choice.
We must take what's good from both,
And heed the people's voice.

Too many shops can spoil a town,
Can take away its soul.
We want the character to stay,
And benefit the whole.

S E Teasdale

MEMORY SMELLS

Ah, the smells of old England are numerous to add,
Sunday roast beef, fresh greens and Yorkshire pud.
Reminds one of youth and times you were glad,
To be part of this ambience, you knew and understood.

Days at the seaside, yearning to taste traditional fish and chips,
To walk along the beach, feel damp salty air and sand in your toes.
Along the promenade and on to the pier, the place for candy floss whips,
Noticing only then, remnants of vinegar stained on your clothes!

A visit to the shops for the odd souvenir, the aroma of fresh bread,
Hot pies, pasties and savouries, the inevitable cream tea
Tell-tale hunger pangs that are always rumbling ahead
So what, you over-indulge but it's that fresh air, sun and sea!

Into the evening, a perchance stop at the *local*
Usually close to the scent of mown grass from the cricket pitch
Sitting outside with crisps and a beer and a chat with a yokel
Tired but replenished, happy yet sad because it's ending again
without a hitch.

So don't forget the good old times and the nicest of smells
Because it's part of your heritage and life that you timed
To be joyful experiences and this always tells
That you really enjoyed them so they're now locked in your mind.

R Partridge

THE OLD SCHOOL BELL AT 'DEERHURST' (GLOS)

I can hear it softly ringing now
Or maybe I dream, who can tell?
But the sound that I hear as I close my eyes
Is the call of the old school bell
For me it's the sound of my childhood
Oh so many years ago
All mixed up with fancies and fairies and fears
And a *sampler* that just wouldn't grow
Slates with a squeaky pencil
And letters that just won't come right
And boots and buttons and clean pinafores
And petticoats starchy and white
The walk down the village lane in the sun
Of a long long summer's day
And a bunch of bluebells to give to *miss*
Gathered along the way
And the bell still rang as the years flew by
Until at last I was grown
And I answered its call oh so many times
With children then of my own
I sit long hours at my window now
While the memories of youth cast their spell
And my grandchildren wave as they run to obey
The summons of the bell
And when God calls, as I know He must
And takes me with Him to dwell
I shall hear on my last long journey
The sound of the old school bell.

Valerie Hibberd

PAST MOMENTS

The living moment becomes the past in one tick of time,
So did we live it to the full by that hourly chime,
We might have cleaned the windows, perhaps gone to see a mate,
Cooked, washed, ironed, and scrubbed the floor before the change of date.
Did we convey a kindly word, or do a thankless task,
Speak to someone we did not like, our face behind a mask.
Tomorrow becomes yesterday all to quick - think on,
Not covering what you set to do, then that time has gone,
There's surely many tomorrows for us to rise and shine,
But to hold very pleasant memories, that would be just fine.

Joan Bowes

THE PENSIONER

The pensioner in his chair doth sit,
with a lovely smile, full of wit.
He's been through life with work and toil,
now has time to sit awhile.
Thinking of days gone by,
or what might have been.
He's seen strife, happy days,
Friends passed on,
his memories linger on
He loves to chat of days gone by,
For him, his memories will never die.

Margaret Brown

INFORMATION

We hope you have enjoyed reading this book - and that you will continue to enjoy it in the coming years.

If you like reading and writing poetry drop us a line, or give us a call, and we'll send you a free information pack.

Write to

Anchor Books Information
1-2 Wainman Road
Woodston
Peterborough
PE2 7BU